THE ROUGH GUIDE TO

Acoustic Guitar

Written by

Hugo Pinksterboer

ROUGH
GUIDES

THE ESSENTIAL TIPBOOK

Rough Guide Tipbook Credits

Journalist, writer and musician **Hugo Pinksterboer** has written hundreds of articles and reviews for international music magazines. He is the author of the reference work for cymbals (*The Cymbal Book*, Hal Leonard, US) and has written and developed a wide variety of musical manuals and courses.

Illustrator, designer and musician **Gijs Bierenbroodspot** has worked as an art director in magazines and advertising. While searching in vain for information about saxophone mouthpieces he came up with the idea for this series of books on music and musical instruments. Since then, he has created the layout and the illustrations for all of the books.

Acknowledgements

Concept, design and illustrations: Gijs Bierenbroodspot

Translation: MdJ Copy & Translation

Editor: Duncan Harris

IN BRIEF

Have you just started playing? Are you thinking about buying an acoustic guitar? Or do you want to know more about the instrument you already own? Then this book will tell you everything you need to know. You'll read about the names of all the parts and what they do, about lessons and practicing, about strings, bridges and saddles, about tuning, about pickups, about acoustic bass guitars and about the guitar's history. And much, much more.

And then?

Having read this Rough Guide, you'll be able to get the best out of your guitar, to buy the best instrument possible, and to easily grasp any other literature on the subject.

Begin at the beginning

If you have just started playing, or haven't yet begun, pay particular attention to the first four chapters. If you've been playing longer, then you might want to skip ahead to chapter 5.

Glossary

The glossary at the end of the book briefly explains most of the terms you'll come across as a guitar player. It also doubles as an index.

CONTENTS

1. THE ACOUSTIC GUITAR

Guitarists can play a handful of chords to a song, or a virtuoso solo over the foundation of a rock band. They can also play classical concerts, alone or with an orchestra, or accompany a dance group or a choir. From campfires to stadium concerts, in bars and in living rooms, acoustic guitarists show up everywhere – and there are almost as many different sorts of guitars as there are guitarists.

On a guitar, several notes can be played simultaneously (*chords*), so you can easily make music alone, without a band or an accompanist. In this sense it's similar to piano, keyboards and organ, which also allow for playing chords.

Acoustic instruments
Another similarity between acoustic guitars and pianos is that they're both *acoustic* instruments, meaning that they don't require an amplifier. The body acts as a *soundbox*, acoustically 'amplifying' what you play.

You're the singer
Just a few different chords will suffice to play a whole bunch of songs with a singer – and that singer could very well be you. After all, there are lots of singer-guitarists who play entire concerts on their own.

Unplugged
Many rock musicians rediscovered the acoustic guitar when MTV's *Unplugged* series broadcast famous bands and artists performing their music with acoustic steel-string guitars, instead of their usual electric ones.

CHAPTER 1

Classical guitarists

Classical players use different guitars and a different technique. Instead of strumming many strings at once, as you do when playing chords, they pluck the strings individually with their fingers and nails. Also, classical guitarists play sitting down, usually with the instrument on their left upper leg, and with a small *footstool* underneath their left foot. Most non-classical guitarists use their right leg when playing seated.

Differences, differences

Plucking with your fingers sounds completely different from strumming with a *pick*, and there are many other methods too. *Slide guitarists* use a tube on one of their left-hand fingers to slide between different notes and chords. However, even when you hear two guitarists play the same acoustic guitar the same way, you'll hear two different sounds.

A well-liked instrument

You'll run into acoustic guitars everywhere. It's a popular instrument – and that makes sense. Here's why:
- They're very affordable. **Little money will do** to buy a guitar that you may well enjoy for many years to come. You can, of course, just as easily spend a fortune on one.
- The guitar is **not a difficult instrument** to learn. But that doesn't mean you'll soon be finished learning – it's as hard to master as the piano, saxophone or any other instrument.
- A guitar **weighs next to nothing**, so you can easily take it along everywhere you go.
- Acoustic guitars aren't loud enough to annoy your neighbours, but there's **no need for an amplifier** to hear what you play.

The two main kinds

There are many different kinds of acoustic guitars. The two most common ones are the *classical guitar* and the *steel-string guitar*. Both of them are known by a number of names.

Classical, Spanish or nylon-string guitars

The classical guitar is mainly used to play classical guitar music. Another name for it is *Spanish guitar*, because it was in Spain that the instrument was given its final form. A third name, to distinguish it from its steel-stringed cousin, is *nylon-string guitar*.

A classical, Spanish or nylon-string guitar

Steel-string, western or folk guitars

Steel-string guitars originally came from America. The names *western guitar* and *folk guitar* are also commonly used. They sound louder and brighter than classical guitars.

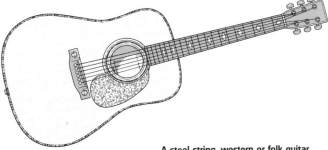

A steel-string, western or folk guitar

And more

There are many more types of acoustic guitars. Twelve-string guitars, for example. Resonator guitars, made to sound a little louder without amplification. Acoustic bass guitars, with four or five strings. And electro-acoustic guitars, which you can hook up to amplifiers just like electric guitars.

Their own sound

All these different guitars have their own individual sound. Some suit a certain style of music, like the flamenco guitar or the jazz guitar, while others suit a certain way of playing, like the twelve-string guitar, which has a broad sound ideal for playing chords.

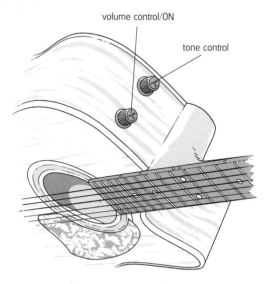

volume control/ON

tone control

You can hook up an electro-acoustic guitar directly to an amplifier

From acoustic to electric

Ever since the 'unplugged' trend, a lot of electric guitarists have returned to acoustic instruments. The opposite, of course, has been going on for much longer – many people start off on an acoustic guitar, and then later switch to an electric one.

2. A QUICK TOUR

From strings, frets and machine heads to necks, waists and heels, acoustic guitars have many different parts. This guided tour will tell you what they're all called, and what they all do.

One look at the *head* or *headstock* will usually tell you whether you're dealing with a classical or a steel-string guitar. If it has two slots, then it's probably a classical guitar. If not, then it's probably a steel-string instrument. Four more differences: classical guitars usually have smaller bodies and wider necks, they lack the *pickguard* that you normally see on steel-string guitars, and the three thinnest strings are made of nylon.

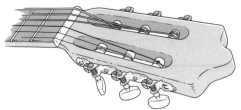

The head of a classical guitar ...

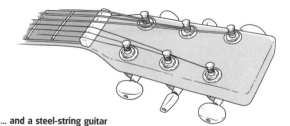

... and a steel-string guitar

5

THE CLASSICAL GUITAR

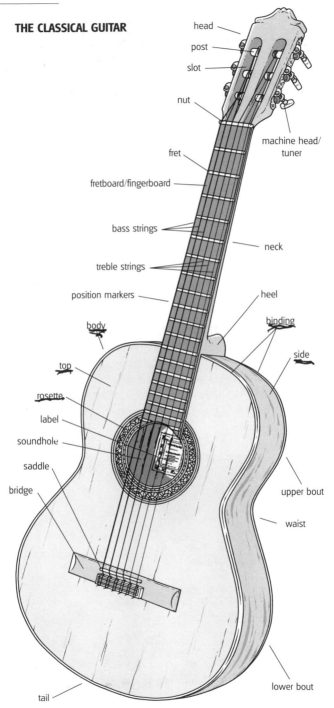

head

post

slot

nut

machine head/tuner

fret

fretboard/fingerboard

bass strings

neck

treble strings

position markers

heel

body

binding

top

side

rosette

label

soundhole

saddle

bridge

upper bout

waist

lower bout

tail

6

The sound

Classical and steel-string guitars also sound different, mainly because of the strings. Classical guitars sound warmer and 'drier' than steel-string guitars, which sound brighter, more penetrating and, of course, more metallic. Also, steel strings project their sound better.

CLASSICAL GUITARS

Classical guitars look quite simple, but they're made of many different parts and are very carefully constructed.

The top

The body's *top* is especially important, as its other name, the *soundboard*, implies. The left side is often the exact mirror image of the right side, in which case it's a *book-matched* top. Between the top and *back* are the *sides* or *rims*.

The soundhole and rosette

The hole in the top is the *soundhole*, and the decoration that surrounds it is the *rosette*. When you look through the soundhole, there's usually a label bearing the name of the brand and the series, or the name and signature of the guitar maker, or *luthier*.

Binding

The *binding* protects and finishes the edges of the body. Some guitars also have bindings around the head and the neck.

The waist and bouts

The broader parts of the body are called the *upper bout* and the *lower bout* or *belly*. In-between is the *waist*.

The heel

The *heel* is the wooden block where the neck is attached to the body.

The fretboard

The strings run along the *fretboard* (which takes its name from the metal frets which run across it). It is also known as the *fingerboard*.

Frets

The thin metal strips, _frets_, which run across the _fretboard_, make a guitar easier to play in tune than a violin, for _example_, which has no _frets_. _Playing at the fourth fret_, or _playing in the fourth position_ means pressing the string down between the third and fourth fret, as close to the fourth as possible. Pressing a string to a fret is known as _fretting_ or _stopping_ the string.

Position markers

On the side of the fretboard that you face while playing, you may find a series of _position markers_ or _markers_. These small dots make it easier to tell which fret is which.

Posts and machine heads

The strings are wound around the _posts_. You tune the guitar by tightening or loosening the strings with the _machine heads_, which are also known as _tuners_ or _tuning machines_.

Strings

The thinnest, highest sounding string is called the _first string_. The thickest string, or the _sixth string_, sounds the lowest. As a reminder, the thinnest string has the thinnest number, 1, and the thickest string has a thick number, 6.

E, A, D, G, B, E

The six strings, from thick to thin, low to high, are tuned to the notes E, A, D, G, B, E. These pitches can be easily memorized as **E**ating **A**nd **D**rinking **G**ives **B**rain **E**nergy.

Wound strings

You can easily see that the thin strings are made of nylon, but the three thickest strings look quite different. They are nylon strings too, but they're wound with very thin metal wire, which explains their name: _wound strings_.

Bass and treble

Wound strings are also known as _bass strings_. The _plain strings_ are also known as _treble strings_ or _melody strings_.

The nut

Coming from the machine heads, the strings first cross the _nut_. This thin strip makes sure that the strings are equally spaced, and that they run at the right height over the fret-board.

The bridge and saddle
At the other end of the guitar, the strings tie around the *bridge*. The light-coloured strip on the bridge, which holds the strings at the right height, is the *saddle*. However, people sometimes use the term 'bridge' to describe either the saddle or the nut.

STEEL-STRING GUITARS
Steel-string guitars exist in many different sizes. Chapters 5 and 13 tell you more about these.

The pickguard
The *pickguard* protects the top from getting scratched by nails and picks when strumming chords – which is what steel-string guitars are most frequently used for.

The fourteenth fret
The body usually starts at the fourteenth fret instead of the twelfth (where it does on classical guitars).

Cutaway
Some steel-string guitars also have a *cutaway*, giving easier access to the highest frets. You'll find two examples on page 28 and 29.

Markers and binding
Steel-string guitars not only have *position markers* on the side of the neck, but on the fretboard too. The *binding* often has a special pattern, such as the popular herringbone.

Plain and wound strings
Most steel-string guitarists use two thin *plain strings* and four thicker *wound strings*, but others use three of each. The standard tuning is identical to that of a nylon-string guitar: E, A, D, G, B, E (from thick to thin, low to high).

The neck and fretboard
The neck of a steel-string guitar is noticeably narrower than that of a classical guitar. Also, the fretboard is slightly

THE STEEL-STRING GUITAR

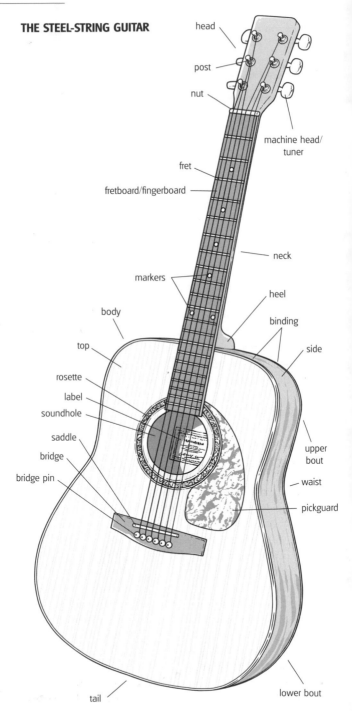

head

post

nut

machine head/
tuner

fret

fretboard/fingerboard

neck

markers

heel

binding

body

side

top

rosette

label

soundhole

saddle

bridge

upper
bout

bridge pin

waist

pickguard

tail

lower bout

rounded, in the same way as a road, being a little bit higher in the middle than at the edges.

The truss rod
Steel strings pull harder than nylon strings. To counteract the extra tension, an adjustable metal *truss rod* is normally built into the neck.

Bridge and bridge pins
The bridge often has a distinctive shape on a steel-string guitar, and the strings are kept in place by *bridge pins* or *pegs*.

The saddle
The saddle of a steel-string guitar is usually not at right angles with the strings, and sometimes consists of two or more parts.

Flattops and archtops
The name *flattop* distinguishes steel-string guitars with a flat top from those with an arched top. *Archtop guitars* look somewhat similar to violins, both because of their curved tops and because they often have two *f*-shaped soundholes.

An archtop with *f*-shaped soundholes

THE INSIDE
Classical and steel-string guitars also differ on the inside. As a player you won't have much to do with this, but you can't open a guitar magazine or book without reading about *braces* – the wooden struts on the underneath of the top.

Bracing
Braces strengthen the top and influence the sound. Most classical guitars have *fan-bracing*, with seven braces laid

out in the shape of a fan. Steel-string guitars, though, have different patterns, and the traditional and most common type is called *X-bracing*, for obvious reasons. Braces against the back are called *ribs* or *struts*.

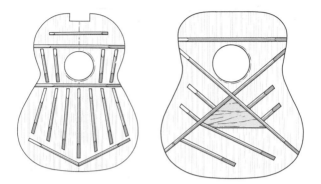

Left: the braces of a classical guitar (fan-bracing); right: the braces of a steel-string guitar (X-bracing).

LEFT-HANDED

Most left-handed guitarists play on a 'right-handed' guitar. After all, your quicker left hand plays at least as big a role as your right hand. If you do want to play left-handed, a classical guitar can be adapted quite easily, although it takes more than just putting the strings on the other way around – the bridge and saddle need to be altered too.

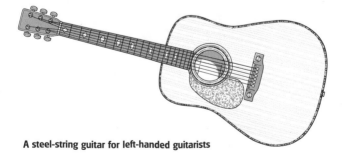

A steel-string guitar for left-handed guitarists

Left-handed guitars

You can't adapt a steel-string guitar in the same way, because the pattern of the braces is different underneath the thick and thin strings. The solution is a left-handed guitar. The range of these guitars is smaller, and you often have to pay a bit more. In most cases the price difference won't be much, but for expensive guitars it may be substantial.

ELECTRO-ACOUSTIC GUITARS

If your guitar isn't as loud as you'd like, you can put a microphone in front of it. Most guitarists, however, prefer a guitar with a built-in *pickup*. This way they can hook up their instrument directly to an amplifier, just like an electric guitar. Acoustic guitars with built-in pickups are called *electro-acoustic guitars*. Usually they are 'regular' steel-string guitars, the pickup being the only difference.

Pickup

A pickup literally 'picks up' the vibrations of the strings, translating them into electric signals which can then be amplified. Most electro-acoustic guitars have a so-called *piezo pickup*, invisibly mounted under the saddle.

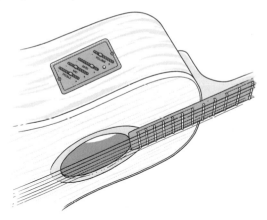

The controls are usually located on the upper bout of the guitar

Controls

The controls for volume and tone are usually located on the upper bout of the guitar, invisible to the audience. They operate the built-in *pre-amplifier* or *pre-amp*, which boosts the signal before sending it out to the main amp. For more information about electro-acoustic guitars, turn to chapter 6.

3. LEARNING TO PLAY

Is it hard to play the guitar? That depends on what you want to do. You can learn the chords to a couple of songs in a few weeks. But what if you want to play classical music, or more than a couple of chords? This chapter focuses on the different ways of reading music, lessons and practicing.

Many famous songs in lots of different styles consist of only three or four chords (notes played simultaneously). Once you learn these chords by heart and practice them for a couple of weeks, you'll be able to play plenty of tunes.

Different styles
Using chords is the easiest way to play the guitar. If you want to play other styles, like classical music or *finger-picking*, it will take longer before you're able to perform an entire piece of music, because your right hand is required to do more, and you'll play both a melody and a bass line at the same time.

GUITAR MUSIC ON PAPER
To play most classical pieces you'll need to be able to 'read music', but traditional notation isn't the only way to put guitar music on paper. Two other important methods are introduced below.

Chord charts
A book with *chord charts* will take you a long way, even without a teacher. Chord charts, such as the one shown

below, simply indicate which fingers are used to stop which strings at which frets to achieve any chord. Once you understand chord charts, you'll find it easy to learn new tunes from song books. Here's how they work:

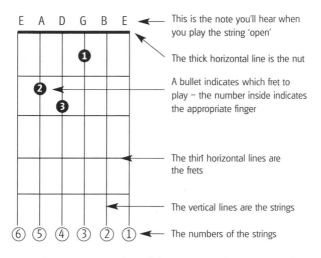

E A D G B E ← This is the note you'll hear when you play the string 'open'

The thick horizontal line is the nut

A bullet indicates which fret to play – the number inside indicates the appropriate finger

The thin horizontal lines are the frets

The vertical lines are the strings

⑥ ⑤ ④ ③ ② ① ← The numbers of the strings

Your fingers are numbered from 1 to 4, from your index finger to your little finger. So, the above example tells you to play string 3 at the first fret with your index finger, play string 5 at the second fret with your middle finger, and play string 4 at the second fret with your ring finger. The result is an E major chord.

Play some blues

To play some blues, all you need is these three simple chords:

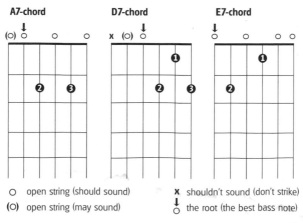

A7-chord   **D7-chord**   **E7-chord**

○ open string (should sound)   x shouldn't sound (don't strike)

(○) open string (may sound)   the root (the best bass note)

15

Play them in this order: 4xA7 2xD7 2xA7 1xE7 1xD7 1xA7 1xE7. Repeat this until you want to finish, but on the last time you play the sequence, change the last chord to an A7 (so then you play 4xA7 2xD7 2xA7 1xE7 1xD7 2xA7). This is called '12-bar blues'.

Tablature

Another way of putting music on paper is the *tablature* (or *tab*) system, which is often used to notate guitar solos and bass lines in song books and magazines. Often the 'regular' way of writing the passage is also included (above or below) because tablature doesn't indicate precise rhythm. Exercise books in tablature are also available. The tablature staff represents a guitar neck, here's how the system works:

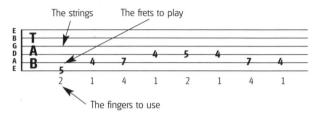

The six horizontal lines represent the six strings, and the numbers on the lines tell you which frets to play. If there are also numbers underneath the lines, they tell you which finger you should use to fret each note. Try playing the above example – if you repeat it you should get a boogie-woogie bass line.

Reading music

Apart from classical players, most guitarists, including fa-mous ones, don't read music, apart from chords and tab. So why would you learn, if classical music isn't your thing? Here are some of the advantages:

• You'll have access to **loads of books and magazines** with exercises, songs and solos, not all of which will be also offered in tablature.

• It will give you **a better insight** into the way chords and songs are structured.

• It enables you to **put down on paper** your own songs, solos, ideas and exercises.

• It allows you to **learn new material very quickly**.

• And finally: learning to read music **isn't that hard at all**.

LESSONS

Hardly anybody learns to play classical guitar music without taking lessons, as it's very hard to master the classical guitar technique on your own.

For other types of music, consulting a teacher isn't such a bad idea either. Of course you can find out everything on your own, but why should you, when there are people who can help you? You could consider getting a few lessons, just to cover the basics, so that at least you start out the right way. Again, there are plenty of famous guitarists who wouldn't know what a music teacher looks like, but there are also lots who have had lessons – some of them still do.

Learning more

A good teacher teaches you more, and there's lots to learn too. Good technique, tone and posture, for example. Reading music, tuning and different playing styles. And for the record, classical lessons are a good start, even if you feel you're going to end up playing something completely different.

Questions, questions

If you're enquiring about a teacher, don't only ask how much the lessons cost. Here are some other questions that you might want to ask:

- Is an **introductory lesson** included? This is a good way to find out how well you get on with the teacher, and, for that matter, with the instrument.
- Is the teacher still interested in taking you on as a student if you are just doing it **for the fun of it**, or are you expected to practice for hours every day?
- Do you have to make a large investment in method books right away, or is **course material provided**?
- Can you **record your lessons**, so that you can listen at home to how you sound and to what's been said?
- Are you allowed to fully concentrate on **the style of music** you want to play, or will you be required to learn other styles?
- Is this teacher going to make you **practice scales** for a long time, or will you start straight off on pieces.
- Can the teacher **offer advice** on purchasing an instrument and other gear?

CHAPTER 3

Finding a teacher

Music stores often have private teachers on staff, or they can refer you to one. You could also ask your local Musician's Union, or a music teacher at a high school or music college in your area.

If you see a good local band performing, try asking the guitarist(s) if they take pupils. Also check the classified ads in newspapers, music magazines and supermarket bulletin boards, and try the *Yellow Pages*.

Group or individual tuition?

While most guitar students take individual lessons, you could also opt for group tuition, if it's available in your area. Personal tuition is more expensive, but it can be tailored exactly to your needs. Professional teachers usually charge around £15–30/$20–50 per hour for individual lessons.

Collectives and music schools

You may also want to check whether there are any teacher's collectives or music schools in your vicinity. These may offer you ensemble playing, masterclasses and clinics as well as normal lessons, and are sometimes considerably cheaper.

Get to work

Finally, visit festivals, concerts and sessions. Watch and listen to lots of bands and soloists. After all, seeing other musicians at work is one of the best ways to pick up tricks. Living legends or local amateurs – every gig's a learning experience. But the best way to learn to play? Practice.

PRACTICING

You can learn to play without reading notes. Without a teacher, too. But not without practicing.

How long?

How long you need to practice for depends on what it is you want to achieve. Some top musicians have practiced eight hours a day for several years, or even more. And the more time you spend, the faster you learn. Still, just half an hour a day should ensure steady progress.

Keep at it

At first, playing can be quite uncomfortable – especially for your left hand, which does a lot of work in what initially seems like a very awkward position. On a steel-string guitar you'll also feel the strings cutting into your fingertips. Keep at it – this will all pass.

Acoustic first

Playing an acoustic guitar is different to playing an electric one. It's harder to press down the strings, and it takes more effort to make it sound really good. However, an acoustic guitar is the best type to start out on, because once you can play an acoustic, then playing an electric will only seem easier, and you'll be able to switch between the two.

Books, videos, CDs and CD-ROMs

There's loads of practice and reading material available for guitarists:

- There are many sorts of **music, tab and song books**, from those for absolute beginners to those for seasoned pros. Many of them come with tapes or CDs of examples and play-along exercises, which often provide a backing band and let you play the tune or solo.
- Most **guitar and music magazines** offer charts, transcriptions and practicing material.
- Lots of well-known guitarists have made **tutor videos**. These video lessons usually last between thirty and ninety minutes, and sometimes come with transcriptions of the exercises.
- There are CD-ROMs that turn your computer into a guitar teacher – and there are even lessons available on the Internet.

Keeping time

You are usually supposed to end a piece at the same tempo that it started at. Therefore it's good to practice occasionally with a *metronome*. It's a small device that ticks or beeps out a steady, adjustable pulse, helping you to work on your tempo, timing and rhythm skills.

Electronics and computers

A *drum machine* is a great alternative to a metronome, and it can give you a whole drum pattern to play along to. And

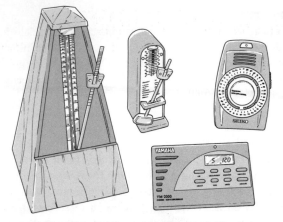

Two mechanical (wind-up) metronomes and two electronic ones

there are also machines, as well as software programs, that accompany you with bass lines, chords or even an entire electronic band. *Phrase trainers* are devices that can slow down a musical phrase from a CD, for example, so you can figure out even the meanest, fastest licks at your own tempo (you can also get software that does this).

4. BUYING A GUITAR

One of the nice things about guitars is that you can buy a pretty good instrument very cheaply, but you can also choose to spend half a year's wages on one. The following chapter tells you everything you need to know before going out to buy an instrument. Chapters 5 and 6 deal with the things you should pay attention to once you're in the shop.

Around £65/$75 is all you need to buy a brand new nylon-string guitar. This isn't much money, when you consider that the instrument has to be made, shipped and sold for it – so don't expect too much. A top-of-the-range guitar can easily cost a hundred times that much, or more.

A little more money
Most teachers will advice you not to begin with the cheapest guitar available, because a little more money will often get you a much better instrument. Try to go for one with a solid top (see page 29); these usually start at around £150/$200.

Steel-string guitars
A decent steel-string guitar will often cost a little more than a classical guitar of similar quality. One reason is that it has to be built to withstand the higher tension of the steel strings.

Bargains
A good thing about buying acoustic guitars is that you sometimes come across some great bargains: guitars that

sound as if they're worth twice or three times as much as their actual price. Of course you need to be able to recognize such instruments, so when you go out to buy your first guitar, take another guitarist along – preferably a good one, who can spot both the good and the bad deals.

Why an expensive one?

The differences between low-budget and expensive guitars aren't always obvious, so what exactly are you paying for when you buy an expensive one?

An intricately inlaid rosette on a classical guitar

Most importantly, better wood and therefore a better sound. Also, higher-quality finish and parts, such as the machine heads, so your guitar will stay in tune for longer. You also pay more for things that don't do anything to the instrument's sound, but a lot to its exclusivity and beauty. An intricate, finely inlaid rosette, for example, or on a steel-string guitar, beautifully designed and worked-out position markers instead of basic dots.

Handmade

Even quite cheap guitars are often sold as 'handmade', but the term can mean many different things. Many low-budget Spanish guitars, for example, are indeed built by hand, but in large factories with conveyer-belt systems. When people talk about 'real' handmade guitars, they are usually referring to those made by proper luthiers, who select and combine all of the individual woods for their particular sound and colour. Conversely, there are very expensive guitars made by manufacturers who proudly describe their extensive use of machines, claiming that they allow for greater precision and consistency than human hands.

Concert guitars and student guitars

Real *concert guitars* are the best quality instruments produced by a luthier, but many budget brands give even their cheapest, mass-produced models the same name. Most luthiers also make *student guitars*, which are cheaper than concert guitars but can still cost well over £1000/$1500.

Bad guitars

You don't come across really bad guitars that often, but they do exist. Guitars with a bent neck, a sagging top, buzzing braces or badly laid frets, for example, should always be avoided. For a little more money – or by looking around for slightly longer – you should be able to buy one that sounds and feels much better.

USED GUITARS

A used guitar usually costs between half and two-thirds of its original price. For that kind of money it should be in good playing condition. And, just like with new guitars, those by well-known brands sell for far more than equally good ones by lesser-known brands.

Shop or private sale?

Purchasing a used instrument privately, from an individual, may be cheaper than buying the same instrument from a shop. However, shops do have their advantages: you can go back, for example, if you have any questions, and you may well get a guarantee. Another difference is that good dealers won't ask an outrageous price, whereas private sellers might, either because they don't know any better or because they think that you don't.

A selection

The other advantage of purchasing from a shop is the selection they offer. Choosing a good instrument usually involves comparing lots of alternatives, so a wide selection is exactly what you need. It's also important to go to lots of different shops and meet lots of knowledgeable sales-people, since they will each have their own 'sound' too.

Take your time

Finally, take your time when buying an instrument – you'll have to live with it for years. However, you may run into an instrument that you fall in love with right away. More often than not it happens to be the guitar you're really looking for. And more often than not it's far too expensive!

MORE INFORMATION

If you want to know more, then get yourself stocked up with guitar magazines, which offer reviews of the latest gear. Also, pick up brochures and catalogues, although make sure you get the price lists to go with them, because as well as providing you with lots of information, they are designed to make you spend more than you meant to. The Internet is another good source for up-to-date product information, and of course there are loads of other guitar books too. More about these resources can be found on pages 115 and 116.

Fairs and conventions

One last tip: if a music *trade show* or *convention* has been organized in your area, go and check it out. Besides all of the instruments that you can try out and compare, you will also meet plenty of product specialists as well as lots of fellow guitar players, who are often an excellent source of information and independent advice.

5. A GOOD GUITAR

Once you know what to look for and listen for, the differences between one guitar and another become much clearer. This chapter describes the technical aspects of the instrument, including the types of woods, varnish and hardware used, and the way they affect the sound. With this information, you're set to buy the best guitar possible.

This chapter starts with a closer look at the instrument, and from page 40 onwards deals with what to listen for. Chapters 7 and 8 are dedicated to the strings, which also play a major role.

WHAT TO LOOK FOR

Most classical guitars look very similar, but steel-string instruments vary considerably. Besides numerous sizes and colours, you'll also find different types of varnish (high-gloss,

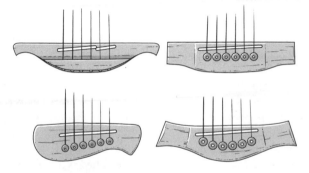

A variety of bridge designs

silk-gloss and matt for example) and a wide variety of pickguard, head, marker, binding and bridge designs.

Varnish
Check that the *varnish* has been applied evenly, and that there aren't any bubbles, stripes or drips. Try to avoid very thickly applied varnish, since too much will restrict the guitar's sound rather than improve it. For a gloss coat, look at the reflection too, which will tell you how well the various coats have been polished.

Inlays
Classical guitars often have more intricately worked rosettes than steel-string instruments. Some inexpensive ones have the rosette glued on instead of inlaid. The markers on the fretboard of steel-string guitars vary from simple dots to elaborate *abalone* (mother-of-pearl) inlays.

Loose parts
Pay attention to how neatly the strings have been fitted; if loose ends are sticking out in all directions, you may wonder how much time and care has gone into the instrument's construction.

Zips and buckles
One more tip before you start play-testing guitars: always be careful not to scratch the varnish with buckles, zips, buttons or bracelets. Good quality classical guitars are especially easy to damage.

THE BODY
The body of a guitar greatly affects the sound. Its size, for one, is a significant factor with steel-string guitars, although classical guitars are pretty much all the same size.

The bigger, the bigger
The basic rule is very simple – a bigger body gives a bigger sound. It gives more volume, richness, depth and low end.

Jumbos and Dreadnoughts
The biggest steel-string guitars are described as *Jumbos* and *Dreadnoughts*. The lower bout of a Jumbo or Jumbo-like

model is often two or three inches wider than that of a classical guitar. The major difference between a Jumbo and a Dreadnought is the bigger waist of the latter, as shown in the picture. In chapter 13 you'll find some of the other standard types and sizes.

A Dreadnought and a Jumbo

Strumming and picking

Large steel-string guitars are usually used for playing chords (*strumming*). Guitars with smaller bodies are often used for fingerpicking, where the thumb plays the bass line and the other fingers play the accompaniment and melody – this is quite similar to classical technique.

Fibreglass body

First introduced by the Ovation brand, guitars with round, fibreglass backs are appropriately known as *roundbacks*. There are roundbacks with nylon and steel strings, with deep and shallow bodies, and also with bodies made of other materials. Roundbacks have a very specific sound, and they're almost always electro-acoustic instruments.

A roundback

Children's guitars

Young players can start out on a *three-quarter-size* or *half-size guitar*, or on an even smaller model. Most children's guitars are nylon-string instruments, but small steel-string guitars are also available. Using the standard tuning, the strings of such instruments will have a low tension (especially with nylon strings). This makes the guitar easier to play, but it also makes it easier to inadvertently bend the strings and therefore play out of tune. Tuning the guitar a fourth or a fifth higher raises the tension and solves this problem (the low E then becomes an A or a B respectively).

Professional small guitars

There are also professional small guitars. Two examples are the *requinto* and the *parlor guitar*, both of which are tuned a bit higher than regular-sized instruments.

Cutaways

A so-called *cutaway*, a section removed from the upper bout, makes it easier to play the higher frets, and some brands offer certain models with or without a cutaway. It is sometimes said that because cutaways make the body asymmetrical, then they kill some of the breadth of an instrument's sound, but many players claim that they make no difference. Either way, any effect on the sound is extremely small.

Venetian

Some cutaways end in a sharp point, while others are more rounded. Sharp cutaways are called *Florentine*, rounded ones *Venetian*.

A Florentine cutaway

A Venetian cutaway

Guitar straps

If you intend to play your guitar standing up, then don't just try it out sitting down – attach a strap so you can see how it feels in both positions. So that they balance correctly, most steel-string guitars have only one *strap button* (the thing you attach the strap to), at the tail. The other end of the strap is tied, using the accompanying leather lace, around the head, just above the nut and under the strings. Never attach a strap to a machine head, as you could easily bend it. A second strap button (or *strap peg*) can be screwed into the heel, but you should probably have a specialist do it. Nylon-string guitars don't have strap buttons, because classical guitarists play sitting down – you can get straps that clip onto the soundhole, but they don't support the guitar very well.

TOP AND INSIDE

The strings make the top vibrate, and these vibrations largely determine the sound of a guitar. This is what makes the top one of the most important parts of the instrument – and it explains why it's also known as the soundboard.

Solid or not

Guitars have either a *solid* or a *laminated top*. A solid top usually consists of two pieces cut from a single block of wood. A laminated top is made of plywood – a number of thin plys of wood glued together.

More responsive

A solid-top guitar responds better to how loudly or softly you play, and to how (nails or pick) and where (at the bridge or at the neck) you strike the string, for example. Guitars with laminated tops often have a bit less life to them, and produce a shallower and less dynamic sound. Solid top classical guitars usually start at around £150/$200. The prices of solid-top steel-string guitars are often a bit higher.

The edge of the soundhole
You can recognize a solid top by looking at the edge of the soundhole. If the grain of the top runs over the edge then it's solid wood.

Slightly round top
While you're looking at the top, also look at it sideways, from a little distance. A good top is very slightly rounded, though this is hardly visible. Guitars with clearly convex tops are usually best avoided, and the same goes for those with sagging, concave tops.

Cedar or spruce
Most guitar tops are made of either *cedar* or *spruce*. Both trees are conifers, yet their woods have different character-istics. In terms of appearance, cedar is usually brown, while spruce has a much lighter, almost white, tint.

Their sounds
Most guitarists agree that cedar tops create a slightly warmer, deeper and rounder sound, and that spruce tops sound a little brighter. Spruce is used more often on steel-string guitars and flamenco guitars, which need a penetrating, more aggressive type of sound. Especially popular among steel-string guitar luthiers is American or Canadian *sitka spruce*. Cedar is more commonly found on classical guitars, although certain types of spruce, such as the European Alpine variety, are often used too.

No two trees
Of course one spruce or cedar top isn't like another, just as no two trees are ever quite the same. There is higher and lesser quality wood of any one kind, and wood can differ in the way it has been cured before use. At the end of the day, the sound is much more important than the type of wood.

Inside and out
Take a good look at the body, both inside and out, to see how well it has been finished. If the inside has a lot of scratches, bad joins or big daubs of glue or varnish, you might wonder if enough attention has been paid to the rest of the instrument. Check whether the neck and fretboard connect seamlessly to the body.

Braces and the rest
There are lots of things that determine a guitar's sound – the shape of the braces, the grain of the top and the material of the back and the sides to name a few. In the end, of course, you'll buy a guitar for its sound, and not for any individual feature. If, however, you want to know more about these technical details, turn to the end of this chapter.

A GOOD NECK, A GOOD FRETBOARD
The neck and fretboard are important to how a guitar plays and feels, and to some extent affect the sound too.

A hard fretboard
The fretboard is made of a hard type of wood. On cheaper guitars it's usually dark-brown rosewood; on more expensive guitars, the harder, near-black ebony is a popular choice. A harder fretboard allows for a brighter and more direct tone, and often has a smoother feel to it too. There should never be any knots or cracks on the fretboard.

A straight neck
The neck should not be curved to the left or right. Check this by looking downwards from the head along the side of the fretboard towards the body. From here you should also be able to see whether the neck is twisted at all.

Concave and convex
The neck and fretboard should be very slightly concave, between the head and the body. To check this, press the low E-string at both the first and the fifteenth fret. The middle of the string should then hang just a little above the frets in the middle of the neck. If it doesn't, then it's a flat neck, or even a convex one, which may result in strings rattling against the frets. If there's more than about 1/32" (1mm)

between the string and the frets, the neck is too concave, and the guitar will be hard to play. Most steel-string guitars allow for neck adjustments with a built-in truss rod, but classical guitars don't.

A third hand

If you're unable to see whether the string touches the frets or not, then ask somebody to gently strike it somewhere in the middle. If the string rings, then the neck must be slightly concave, which is exactly what you want.

Intonation

At the twelfth fret, the strings should sound exactly one octave higher than when they're open (when you don't fret them). If they do, then the *intonation* of the guitar is correctly set up. To check, place a finger very softly on the thick E-string, exactly above the twelfth fret, barely touching it, and then strike the string pretty hard, and close to the bridge, with your other hand. What you'll hear – with a little practice – is a high, thin tone known as a *harmonic* (or sometimes *overtone* or *flageolet*). Now press the same string to the twelfth fret, as you would in normal playing, and you should get exactly the same pitch. Check the other strings in the same way.

The twelfth fret

On a classical guitar, the neck and the body meet underneath the twelfth fret. On steel-string guitars they usually meet under the fourteenth fret. On both types of instrument, the twelfth fret is usually highlighted with a double dot or an extra big marker.

Hard to hear

Especially when you're just starting to play, it may be difficult to hear whether a harmonic sounds too high, too low or just right. An electronic tuner (see pages 75–76) can help, but asking an experienced guitarist will probably be even more effective.

A different pitch

If the intonation is bad, then the notes which you play on the lower frets will be out of tune with those played on the higher frets. This is bad enough when you play on your own, but the effect is even more noticeable when you play with others. Also, with such a guitar, there's a risk that your ears will slowly get used to the wrong pitches, and then when you switch to a good guitar, it may sound out of tune – to you.

Decent strings

The cause of an intonation problem is often bad strings rather than a bad guitar. Some cheaper, but perfectly good, instruments are sold with strings that simply don't allow for proper intonation. A set of decent strings, which won't cost much, may well solve the problem and will also improve the sound.

Dead spots

Another important test is to check the instrument for *dead spots*. Play all the strings at every fret and check that there are no positions where the sound is noticeably shorter, drier or softer.

Rattles

You should also check for rattles and buzzing sounds – especially on used guitars. Some unwanted noises may only be noticeable at certain pitches. Harmonics, which you can also play at a number of different frets (the fifth and the seventh, for example), can sometimes make otherwise inaudible sounds stand out. Another test is to gently tap the body with a fingertip or a knuckle, and listen.

If something is really loose, you may find out by carefully shaking the guitar. If you want to know more about rattles and buzzes, and where they may come from, then turn to page 42.

MORE NECKS

Broad necks, narrow necks, long necks and short necks; again, there are more variations for steel-string instruments, but there's plenty to know about the necks of classical guitars too.

Classical guitar necks

Classical guitars have quite wide fretboards, measuring a little over two inches (5cm) at the nut. The strings are quite far apart from one another, allowing for the techniques used in classical guitar music. When you're just starting out, a slightly narrower neck will be easier to play, but you'll find that there isn't much variation between different instruments.

The thumb

Proper classical guitar technique requires you to rest the thumb of your left hand somewhere in the middle of the back of the neck. The neck has been designed for this purpose.

Classical left-hand position

Steel-string necks

The necks of most steel-string guitars have been designed to make fingering chords easier, and most players put their thumb higher on the back of the neck than classical players.

D, C and V

The letters D, C and V are used to describe the different shapes of steel-string guitar necks: a neck with a D-profile has a rather flat back, while the letter C is used to indicate a rounder profile. Necks with a 'sharper' V-profile are used mainly by guitarists who fret the sixth string, or even the fifth string, with their left-hand thumb – the slightly pointed back allows the thumb to fit more easily around the neck. Fingerpickers tend to like V-profiles.

Radius

The fretboards of steel-string guitars (and most electric guitars) are a bit higher in the middle than under the E-strings. This curve, called the *radius* or *camber*, makes it easier to finger chords. The radius is expressed in inches, and the higher the number, the flatter the fretboard. Most steel-string guitars have a radius of twelve inches. A neck with a *compound radius* is a bit rounder at the nut than at the last fret.

Neck widths

Steel-string guitar necks are usually between 1 11/16" and 1 13/16" wide at the nut (42–46mm), and about 7/16" (1cm) more at the twelfth fret. If you mainly play chords, a narrower fretboard is easier. For other playing techniques, like fingerpicking, many guitarists prefer a wider neck.

The scale

When an open string is struck, it vibrates between the nut and the saddle. On one guitar that distance may be bigger than on another. In technical terms, the first guitar would be said to have a longer *scale*. On steel-string guitars the scale varies from a little under 25" to about 26" (62.5–65cm). Classical guitars usually have a scale of slightly less than 26".

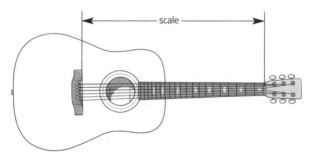

The scale is the length of the strings measured from the saddle to the nut

More tension

The longer the scale, the further apart the frets will be, and so the more you have to spread your fingers. Also, the strings have to be wound a little tighter to sound the same pitch. This increased tension helps produce a broader, fuller sound and a little bit more volume. Fingerpicking guitarists often choose guitars with longer scales.

Acoustic bass guitars

Most acoustic bass guitars have four strings, which are tuned E, A, D and G (the same notes as the four thickest

guitar strings, but one octave lower). Short strings can't go that low and still sound good, which is why bass guitars have much longer scales – often up to 34" (85cm).

Children's guitars

A classical three-quarter-size guitar has a scale of slightly less than 23" (57cm), and a half-size guitar has one of about 21"(53cm). The scale of the smallest children's guitars is as little as 16" (40cm).

A choice of necks

If you've found a great guitar but you don't like the neck, there's usually not much you can do. Some expensive models, though, come with a choice of necks.

Acoustic bass guitars have very long scales

Electric-style acoustics

You can get acoustic steel-string guitars that have been designed specifically for electric guitarists. Like electric guitars they have very narrow necks, and strings just above the fretboard, making it easier to switch between the two.

ACTION

The *action* of a guitar refers to the distance between the strings and the fretboard. The higher the action, the bigger the distance.

Too high, too low

A guitar with a high action is harder to play, since you have to press the strings down further. If the action is too low, though, the strings may rattle against the frets. Flamenco guitarists often produce that rattling sound, intentionally playing with a very low action and strumming the strings very hard.

From high to low

On new guitars the action is more often on the high than

on the low side. This makes sense, because it's easier to lower a high action than it is to raise a low one. An over-high action can also be remedied temporarily, when you're trying out a guitar.

Capos

Capos are special clamps that you can mount at any fret on the neck, changing the pitch of the instrument. However, they also lower the action, and so they can be useful if you're play-testing a guitar which has a higher action than you'd like. You can put a capo on the first fret, and although everything will sound a semitone/half-step higher, you should be able to judge what the guitar would feel like if you were to have the action adjusted.

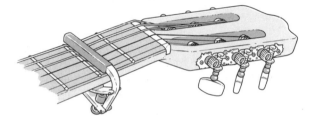

A capo, shown here on the second fret

Adjusting the action

A repairer can adjust the action by altering or changing the nut or saddle (or both). The truss rod may also be adjusted.

Nylon-string action

A classical guitar is considered to have a low action if the distance between the twelfth fret and the bottom of the thick E-string is about 9/64" (3.5mm) or less. If there's more than about 3/16" (4.5mm), the action is considered to be high. There are great classical guitars, however, with an action 4/16" or more. The action on the low E-string is usually a bit higher than on the high E-string, because the thick strings need more space to vibrate. If the overall action is too low, the sound may suffer.

Steel-string action

Steel-string guitars have a lower overall action. Usually there's about 1/16" (1.5mm) under the high E and slightly more under the low E (around 5/64" or 2mm).

METAL AND BONE

The main non-wood parts of a guitar are the machine heads, the frets, the nut and the saddle. Even these small components contribute to the sound, the playability and the appearance of an instrument.

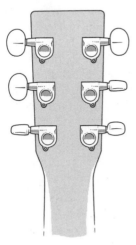

Machine heads

Good machine heads wind easily and smoothly, and don't rattle. On classical guitars they're always open, while on most steel-string guitars they're enclosed, sealed by a metal housing. This type is usually self-lubricating, so there's no need to oil them.

Enclosed machine heads on a steel-string guitar

Gear ratios

Machine heads also come in different 'gears'. If you have 10:1 machine heads, the posts that wind the strings turn around once for every ten times you turn the key. Tuning is easier and more precise with a ratio of 14:1 or even 16:1. If you find a great guitar, but you're not happy about the machine heads, they can be easily replaced.

All that glitters...

Many steel-string guitars have gold-coloured machine heads instead of chrome-plated ones. The gold tint is often brass, but real gold-plated ones are also available, and they're less expensive than you might expect.

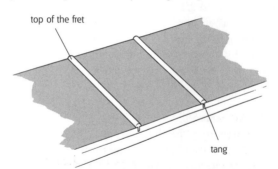

top of the fret

tang

Frets

Smooth and well-finished frets make for a guitar that sounds good and plays well. If the frets are slightly too short, the E-strings may sometimes slip off the edge of the fretboard. If they're too long, and jut out from the neck, it may indicate that the guitar has been stored in too dry an environment (see page 85).

Fretless basses

There are acoustic bass guitars that have fretless necks, just like double basses. They sound a bit more melodious (they 'sing' more, some say) and it's much harder to learn to play them in tune – again like double basses. Fretless guitars are extremely rare.

Two-octave fretboards

Nylon-string guitars usually have eighteen or nineteen frets. In addition, they sometimes have one or two half-frets beside the soundhole, for the very highest notes. Steel-string guitars usually have twenty frets, but on some you'll find up to twenty-four for the highest two strings. On these strings you can then play two whole octaves, but it's difficult to make it sound very good.

Saddles and nuts

Saddles and nuts used to be made of ivory, but now they're generally made of a hard synthetic material designed to transfer the vibrations from the strings to the top as well as possible. Saddles and nuts made of bone are sometimes found on more expensive guitars (around £350/$500 and up).

Compensated saddles

Unlike classical guitars, steel-string instruments often have a *compensated saddle* – one that is not at a 90° angle with the strings. Compensated saddles are designed to improve a guitar's intonation, making it sound in tune in every posi- tion. Some saddles even consist of two or more parts, for the same purpose.

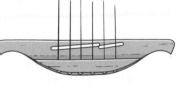

A compensated saddle

The grooves in the nut

If you're trying out a guitar and the strings keep getting stuck during tuning, then the grooves in the nut might be too narrow. A temporary solution is to repeatedly press the string just behind the nut as you're tuning; a permanent solution is to have the nut adjusted or replaced.

WHAT TO LISTEN FOR

There's lots to listen out for when testing guitars – both good and bad things. Here are some tips for judging guitars with your ears.

The player

How a guitar sounds depends on who's playing it. If you don't play yet, or haven't been playing for long, then you won't be able to get the most out of an instrument. If you really want to know what it can sound like, have a good guitarist play it – and that might well be the salesperson. When you're listening, try sitting a little distance away from the guitar, as this will allow you to make a better judgement of the instrument's sound.

A wall works well

When you're playing, you don't hear the same as your audience does, because a guitar sounds different from the front. However, you can get a pretty good idea of how an instrument sounds from the listener's position by sitting in front of a wall, so that the sound bounces back to you.

Balance

A good guitar is well balanced, in terms of volume, tone and sustain. The low strings shouldn't be louder than the high ones, nor the other way around. Also, the difference in tone between the wound and the plain strings shouldn't be too pronounced. On nylon-string guitars, the third string (G) often sounds noticeably less bright than the D, which is the first wound string (some strings and string sets have been designed to reduce this effect, see page 53). As for sustain, the thin strings don't ring for as long as the thick ones, and in higher positions the notes don't last as long, but the differences should be slight and evenly gradated.

Dynamics

Something else to check is a guitar's range from loud to soft – its *dynamic* range. A good instrument should have a nice, full tone even at the lowest volume, but should also sound good when played really loudly. The most important thing, of course, is how it sounds at the volume at which you usually play.

Taste

Although some guitars suit one style of music more than another, a guitar's sound is mainly just a matter of taste. You may go for a bright sound, or prefer something warmer. The heavy low strings that you might favour might sound too boomy for another player. Some guitarists like a very transparent sound – so that when you play a chord you can hear every single string separately – while others prefer an instrument with a thicker, denser character.

A shallow sound

Some guitars are less articulate and responsive and have less of a dynamic range than others. These shallow-sounding instruments may not be unpleasant at first, but can become very boring after a while.

Two at a time

When trying to choose the best one out of a large selection of guitars, you'll probably get confused. The best technique is to pick out two guitars and to just compare those. Keep the best one, and then pick a third guitar to compare it to. And so on.

Don't look

When you select the guitars that you're going to try out, you'll almost automatically look at their prices. The chances are that you will then *hear* those prices too. Try to decide what you think of each instrument – by playing it or getting someone else to play it – before you've looked at the price.

Turn around

If you've found a couple of guitars that you like, and you want to compare their sounds, then ask someone to play the same piece of music on each one. If you really only want to go for the sound, and not the looks, then turn around so that you can't see which is being played.

No two are the same
You'll never find two guitars that sound exactly alike. Not even if they're the same brand, the same series and the same colour. So it's best to play the guitar you're going to buy, and to buy the guitar which you played, instead of an 'identical' one from the stockroom.

Electro-acoustic
Many electro-acoustic guitars are simply 'regular' guitars with a built-in pickup, and judging their acoustic properties is no different from judging any other acoustic guitar.

USED INSTRUMENTS
Used guitars require the same tests and checks as new ones, but there are a few things that require extra attention:

- Check the body, the neck and the fretboard for **cracks, fractures and other damage**.
- Damage is not only caused by bumps and falls, but also by sudden changes in **humidity or dry air** (see page 85). Small cracks in the varnish, or frets that jut out from the neck, may indicate that a guitar has been stored in a very dry environment.
- Pay attention to **seams and joints**, for example between the fretboard and body.
- Listen out for things you don't want to hear. Some **rattles or buzzes** may be easily corrected, for example by adjusting the action or even simply tightening a strap button. If a string is broken, its machine head may buzz.
- Other **sounds** you won't be able to get rid of, or you'll need to have them repaired by a specialist. A loose brace, for example, an invisible crack in the body, a broken machine head, or a loose nut or pickguard.
- Finding the **cause of the rattling** is often harder than solving the problem; you can check an entire guitar only to realize that the culprit is a loose winding on one of the strings.
- **Worn-out frets** can make your strings buzz, and make it difficult to bend them. However, frets can always be replaced or refinished.

Bending strings – a tough job with worn-out frets

- Improper intonation may be the result of **an old set of strings**.
- On electro-acoustic guitars, make sure all the **controls** are working well, and don't creak. Creaking is often easily resolved with contact spray, but even then you have to know what you're doing.
- The tiniest drop of oil can make **machine heads** move smoothly again. Inferior or old ones can be replaced, if the guitar is worth it.
- A good used guitar may last for years and years to come.
- Again, **take somebody along** who knows about guitars, especially if you're buying from a private seller.

Vintage instruments

A guitar's sound may well improve with age – especially if it has a solid spruce top – and rare and historical guitars sell for a great deal in specialist shops. However, an older guitar is not necessarily a better guitar.

WHAT, WHERE AND WHY?

To some, only the sound matters, but others like to know about *why* a guitar sounds the way it does – what braces do, for example, or what the grain may say about the quality of the instrument. Here are a few points.

Styles of bracing

Everything that's attached to the top determines how it vibrates. That, in turn, determines the sound of the guitar. A luthier can control the sound by varying the bracing pattern, but also by using thinner, wider, higher, flatter or scalloped braces. Every luthier has their own bracing style.

Grain, thickness and soundholes

The wood of the top, the way it has been sawn, its thickness and its structure are all important factors too. Top-of-the-range instruments often have a thin, *quarter-sawn top*, with fine, even grains and a uniform tint – but there are also first-rate instruments that look nothing like that at all. The sound can also be influenced by the size and placing of the soundhole; some guitars have non-circular or even multiple soundholes.

Not all guitars have only one soundhole (Ovation)

The back and sides

The back and sides are less important than the top, but they still play a significant role. On most guitars these sections are laminated, and guitars with bodies made entirely out of solid wood normally cost over £750/$1000.

Kinds of wood

Mahogany is often used for the backs and sides of inexpensive guitars. A coloured varnish may be used to make it look like the rosewood (*Rio*) that you find on more expensive instruments. Other commonly used types of wood include *maple, nato* and – in the higher price ranges – *walnut* or *koa*.

Varnish

Thick coats of varnish slow down the vibrations of the soundboard. The thinner the varnish, the better a guitar may sound. Until the 1970s, most guitars were finished with cellulose varnish, which is made from natural materials and is said to allow the wood to breathe. Today this type is used only on certain expensive guitars; the majority are finished with a synthetic-based varnish, although alcohol- and water-based versions are also popular.

Even the frets

Every part of a guitar influences the sound – even the frets. Pointed frets make for an edgier tone than rounded ones. However, in the end you should buy a guitar because you like it as a whole and not because of what you think of its separate parts.

Give it time

Finally, remember that a good guitar only starts to sound its best when you play it for about twenty minutes. Many say that only then does an instrument really 'open up', but also it simply takes a little while to get to know a guitar well enough to make it sound like it should.

6. ELECTRO-ACOUSTIC GUITARS

Sometimes you may need a little more volume than an acoustic guitar can offer, especially when you're on stage. That's where electro-acoustic guitars come in – acoustic guitars that can be hooked up directly to amplifiers.

Most electro-acoustic guitars look no different from any other steel-string guitars – they're usually the same instruments, just with some added electronics. The visible difference is a small control panel, usually located on the left upper bout; the invisible difference is the pickup. Most electro-acoustics have a *piezo pickup*, which looks like no more than a thin strip and which hides beneath the saddle.

Pickups and pre-amps

The *pickup* or *transducer* converts the vibrations of the strings into electrical signals. The first stop for these signals

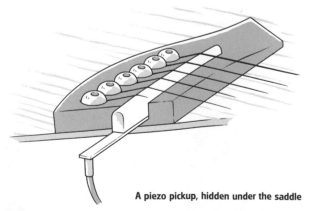

A piezo pickup, hidden under the saddle

is the *pre-amp*, which is usually built into the guitar, boosting the signals before sending them to an external amplifier.

Prices

Electro-acoustic guitars come in a wide variety of price ranges, the cheapest models starting at less than £200/$300. Often you can choose to have a normal or an electro-acoustic version of the same guitar. The latter often costs around £100 300/$150 400 extra, but the difference depends on both the guitar and the pickup/pre-amp combination. Some brands offer you a wide selection of different systems.

Guitar microphones

Many top guitarists combine a piezo pickup with a small microphone in order to achieve a rounder sound. These microphones can either be clipped onto the edge of the soundhole or mounted inside the guitar. When classical players want a bit more volume they often use a clip-on mike. You can also get microphones and cheaper pick-ups that can be glued to the soundboard, but these often yield less satisfying results.

Shallow bodies

There are also electro-acoustic guitars, usually with nylon strings, that are solely built for amplified playing. They usually have a *shallow body* that hardly acts as a soundbox at all, and often have a grille instead of a soundhole. Nylon-string electro-acoustics start at around £350/$500.

Feedback problems and solutions

Electro-acoustic guitars are notorious for causing *feedback* – the same loud screech that you hear if you accidentally hold a microphone in front of a loudspeaker. The larger the guitar's body and the louder you play, the worse the feedback is likely to be. A common solution is a *notch filter*, which may be found on the pre-amp or the external amp. It fights feedback by filtering the problem frequency out of the sound. Also, try simply covering the soundhole; you can get special rubber discs for the purpose, known as *feedback busters*.

Volume, tone and more

The control panel of an electro-acoustic guitar usually features both volume and tone controls, the latter often separated into high/treble and low/bass, just like a home stereo amplifier. Some pre-amps offer other features, such as more extensive tone controls (*equalizers* or *EQs*), built-in effects (such as *reverb*) or an electronic tuner.

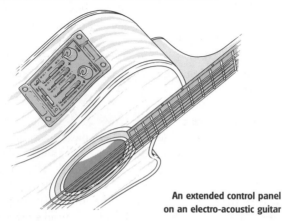

An extended control panel
on an electro-acoustic guitar

Battery check

The pre-amp is usually powered by a battery, and a check light on the control panel informs you about its remaining power. If it's running low, you'll be warned by the sound too, which will get progressively worse and quieter.

Retro-fitting

If you have a normal acoustic guitar, you can have it turned into an electro-acoustic by having a pickup and pre-amp *retro-fitted*, but this job is best left to the specialist. A pick-up that's not properly installed may cause feedback and other problems. The prices of pickups and pre-amps vary a lot, as do the costs of having them installed, but if you want good results expect to spend at least £150/$200 altogether. Some of the well-known brands that make good pickups are Ashworth, EMG, EPM, Fishman, Highlander, L.R. Baggs and Seymour Duncan.

Which guitar?

You can turn basically any guitar into an electro-acoustic one, but a model with quite a small body may sound better and will be less likely to cause feedback.

Once in a while

If your guitar needs to be amplified only once in a while, then a magnetic pickup that you can mount in the sound-hole, using clips, clamps or adhesive tape, may be the best and cheapest option – decent ones start at around £60/$75. Magnetic pickups, though, don't respond at all to nylon strings. And remember, don't replace your nylon strings with steel ones, as this may ruin your instrument.

Normal microphones

Regular microphones are often used to record guitars in studios. On stage, though, they can cause bad feedback, and they force you to keep your guitar very still, aiming the soundhole at the microphone at all times. A clip-on mike, as mentioned above, buys you the freedom to move around, and makes the sound more even.

Acoustic amplifiers

Unlike amplifiers for electric guitars, which greatly contribute to the colour of the overall sound, amps for acoustic guitars are supposed to make an instrument louder without changing its character. These special amps are known as *acoustic amplifiers*, self-contradictory as it may sound. In real terms, you can hook up an acoustic guitar to any amp, but it might not sound quite as clean as you'd like; there are also acoustic/electric amplifiers, designed specifically for use with both sorts of guitar.

Power ratings

The smallest acoustic amps have a power output of about 10–15 watts RMS, which suffices for the very smallest venues only. If you need more power, then expect to pay at least £200/$300 for an amp of approximately 30 watts. If you play in a band with other amplified instruments, you may need 100 watts or more.

Effects

Amps often come with built-in effects. *Reverb*, the most common type, adds a slight echo, making it sound as if you're playing in a church. Also popular is *chorus*, which doubles the sound and gives it a full and spacious feel. These and many other effects are also available in foot- and hand-operated units, specifically designed for acoustic instruments.

Combos

Acoustic amplifiers are usually *combo amplifiers* or *combos*, meaning that they have the amplifier and loudspeaker(s) together in a single unit. Just like home stereo systems, combos each have their own sound, so always try a few out before buying one, and preferably use your own guitar to play-test them.

Buying tips

- Always listen to electro-acoustic guitars **unamplified as well as amplified** (even those with a shallow body).
- The better the instrument, the less its **sound will change** when it's plugged into an amp.
- Electro-acoustic guitars tend to have a **low action and light strings**. You can always change these things later.
- A good guitar won't be too **sensitive to feedback**. Check this out by comparing a couple of guitars – put the instruments at various angles to an amplifier and see which reacts more, but don't turn the volume up too loud…
- Check that the **volume and tone controls** work evenly.
- Check that **the battery** is easily replaceable. If it's not, it can be very inconvenient – especially if it goes during a concert.

7. GOOD STRINGS

Without good strings you'll never get the most out of your instrument. Strings affect both the sound and the feel of the guitar, and there are many types to choose from. This chapter describes the materials, gauges, windings and tensions available, and explains the differences they make.

Strings sound best when you fit them properly, and they'll sound good for longer if you keep them clean. Chapter 8 deals with both these subjects.

A warning
Steel strings put a lot of tension on your guitar – in fact, the equivalent to the weight of a guitarist. Nylon-string guitars are only designed to cope with about half as much tension, so if you put steel strings on a nylon-string instrument, the body may crack, the bridge may come loose, and the neck may warp.

Nylon on steel
Putting nylon strings on a steel-string guitar is not a good idea either. The strings may snap on the sharp corners of the holes in the posts, and will lack the tension required to make the soundboard vibrate sufficiently. So, you probably won't cause any damage to the guitar, but you won't get much sound either.

Which strings?
The only way to find out exactly which brand or series of strings you like best on your guitar is to try lots out,

although a knowledgeable salesperson may be able to suggest a few types if you explain the sort of sound you're looking for.

Cheap strings

As previously mentioned, cheap guitars usually come with cheap strings. By fitting some more expensive ones you can often dramatically improve both the sound and the intonation of such instruments.

NYLON STRINGS

When it comes to nylon strings, you need to know about the various brands, tensions, windings and colours. Here are the basics.

Tensions

Most brands offer three of four choices of string tension, and some offer even more. If you pick *high tension* strings, they will be and feel a little tighter. Playing will be slightly heavier, and the sound will be a bit brighter and more articulate than with *normal* or *low tension* strings. Lower tension strings are easier to play, and they tend to produce a warmer and drier tone.

Why wound strings?

The three thickest strings consist of ultra-fine nylon wires (*floss nylon* or *multi-filaments*) that are twisted together and then wound with metal wire. The winding makes the strings heavier, allowing them to sound lower without losing their brightness. If you were to use plain nylon wire for these strings, they'd have to be very thick, and this would result in a dull, weak tone.

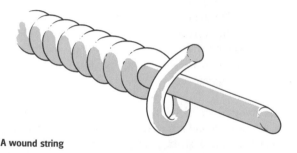

A wound string

The third string

The dullness of thick, plain nylon is demonstrated to some extent by the third string, the G. As the thickest plain string, it tends to sound a bit muddy and lifeless compared to its neighbours – the thinner B-string and the wound D-string. To make the G sound brighter, some brands treat it as a wound string or make it from a special type of nylon.

Silver, bronze or gold-plated

Most wound strings come with a silver-plated brass winding, which gives them a nice, bright tone. Bronze-wound strings are often said to sound a bit warmer (by those who like them) or less bright (by those who don't). Strings with gold-plated brass windings sound good, but gold is quite a soft metal so the brightness doesn't last that long.

Clear, yellow, red or black

Plain strings are usually made of clear transparent nylon, like fishing wire, but yellow, red and black ones are also available. Most experts say that the colour doesn't do anything to the sound, but not everyone agrees.

Prices

A decent set of nylon strings costs about £7/$9. A really good guitar may deserve better strings, and you can spend £12/$15 or more. It may be worthwhile to try such a set, even if it's only once, because you won't know what you're missing until you've given them a try.

Life span – plain strings

Depending on how much you play, good plain strings may not deteriorate much in terms of sound until they're over a year old. There comes a time, though, when they stop tuning properly and the intonation goes off (see page 32). Serious players change their plain strings every month or so.

Life span – wound strings

Wound strings don't keep their tone nearly as long as plain strings. The windings are attacked by sweat, and dirt easily settles in the grooves, resulting in a duller sound. How long that takes depends predominantly on how often you play, but also on such factors as the quality of the strings, how well you keep the strings, and even the acidity of your perspiration (the more acidic it is, the faster the sound will deteriorate). Keen amateur players change their bass strings every few months, but most pros change them about every two weeks. The better your guitar and your playing, the sooner you'll notice a loss of brightness.

Nine in a set
Since it makes sense to replace your wound strings more often than your plain ones, some brands sell sets of nine strings: one of each of the plain ones and two of each of the wound ones. You can also buy strings individually, but it works out slightly more expensive.

Brands
Some of the main nylon string brands are Aranjuez, Augustine, D'Addario, D'Aquisto, La Bella, GHS, Hannabach, Savarez and Thomastik-Infeld.

STEEL STRINGS
Plain steel strings don't differ that much from one brand to another, with the exception of so-called *silver steel strings*, which produce a slightly different tone. On steel-string guitars, the third string is usually wound, but some players prefer a plain one because it's easier to bend.

Bronze windings
On steel strings, you'll rarely find the silver-plated windings that work so well on nylon strings. Bronze is more popular, and gives a bright, open sound.

Phosphor bronze
Strings with phosphor bronze windings are also widely used, although guitarists don't always agree on whether they sound brighter or duller. The only way to find out is to buy a set and try them on your own guitar. After all, the sound of the strings depends on the instrument as much as the sound of the instrument depends on the strings.

Comparing strings
There are lots of other string types too, ranging from those with different windings to those that combine silk and steel in the core. An effective and inexpensive way to compare

two types is to put on a whole new set of strings, but to use one wound string (the D is probably best) of an alternative brand/series.

Gauges

Nylon strings come in various tensions; steel strings come in various *gauges* (thicknesses). The main differences between light- and heavy-gauge strings are shown below:

Lighter strings	Heavier strings
• sound 'lighter' and thinner	• sound 'heavier' and thicker
• don't sustain for long	• sustain for longer
• produce less volume	• produce more volume
• are easier to play and bend	• are more tiring to play
• need to be tuned more often	• don't detune as fast
• break more easily	• last longer

Hundredths of an inch

String gauges are expressed in fractions of an inch. When guitarists speak about the gauge of a set of strings, they always refer to the width of the high E-string. In a 010-set, often just called a 'set of tens', the first string measures 0.010 inches (one-hundredth of an inch/0.25mm). Most steel-string guitar players opt for a 012-set.

Electric players

Most electric guitarists use 010-sets, or even lighter ones, so it can take them a while to get used to the heavier strings of an acoustic. You can use 010s on an acoustic guitar, but most instruments sound better and louder with slightly heavier ones. The heaviest steel-string sets are 014s.

Names

Most brands also use names to indicate the gauges of their string sets. Usually 010s are called *extra light*, 011s are *custom light*, 012s are *light*, 013s are *medium* and 014s are *heavy*, although the names do vary from brand to brand. Different manufacturers also vary the exact gauges of the other strings in the sets.

Heavier strings, higher tension

The heavier a set of strings is, the more tension it puts on an instrument. Replacing your strings with heavier ones may therefore result in a higher action, because the extra tension can pull the neck up a little, or slightly raise the top by pulling at the bridge. This higher action can, of course, be lowered again (see page 37).

Nut problems

The strings of a heavier set may also get caught in the grooves of the nut, making it difficult to tune them properly. The solution is to have the nut replaced or to have the grooves widened.

When to change?

How long a set of steel strings lasts depends on many factors. The biggest is how much and how heavily you play them, but they are also very sensitive to sweat, especially if it's acidic. Many guitarists who want to keep their sound up to scratch change their strings every few weeks, or even more frequently. On the other hand, you may well enjoy a single set for two years or so – but you won't know what you've been missing until you fit some new ones.

Prices and brands

A good set of steel strings costs around £6–9/$8–12. Good strings have a better sound, and keep sounding good for longer. A few well-known steel string brands are D'Addario, D'Aquisto, Dean Markley, DR, Ernie Ball, Gibson, GHS, Kyser, Martin and SIT.

8. CLEANING AND CHANGING STRINGS

This chapter shows you how to maintain and change strings properly, so that they sound as good as possible, for as long as possible. Tuning tips follow in chapter 9.

To maximize the life of your strings, you should take a closer look at your guitar. Firstly, smoother frets don't wear down the strings as quickly. Rough spots can be smoothened, very carefully, with some ultra fine steel wool (number 0000, sold in hardware stores).

The nut and saddle
Check the nut and saddle as well – any sharp edges can cause strings to snap. Fine steel wool, again, or some ultra-fine sandpaper, will usually be all you need to smoothen things up. If you keep breaking the same string, then look to see where it snaps and check for sharp edges there.

Humidity and dirt
Airborne dust, dirt, grease, smoke and moisture, as well as anything on your fingers, can also cause strings to lose their brightness. Wound strings are extra sensitive to this, because they trap lots of particles in their grooves. As a guideline, when strings start to lose their colour, they will need to be changed quite soon. They may not break for another year or two, or even more, but a new set will sound noticeably better.

Clean and dry
An easy way to keep your strings in good condition is to wash your hands and dry them well before playing, and to

clean and dry the strings afterwards. Any lint-free cloth works well – an old T-shirt, for example. Wipe down the tops of the strings, but also pull the cloth between the strings and the fretboard, and run it up and down the neck a couple of times.

String cleansers
If you get very sweaty fingers, you may consider getting some special string cleanser, which removes the dirt from the grooves of your wound strings and also cleans the plain ones. It's not that expensive and a little bottle should last you a long time.

Smoother strings
There are also products that are designed to make your strings feel smoother. They often help to repel dirt as well. There are various brands, such as Finger-Ease and Fast Fret.

Talcum powder
Rubbing your hands with talcum powder reduces perspiration. Don't use too much, though, or the powder might damage the strings. Washing your hands with pH-neutral soap may also limit perspiration.

Spare sets
Old strings are more likely to break than new ones, so the more often you change your strings, the less likely it is that you'll ever snap any. On the other hand, even a brand new string can break, so if you do a gig, be sure to have a spare set with you, or even a spare guitar.

NEW STRINGS
There are lots of ways to fit new strings. If you do it any correct way, the strings will stay in tune well and will be less likely to slip or break. Also, you'll keep them from damaging your guitar. Here's a few general tips, followed by instructions on now to replace nylon strings (page 60) and steel strings (page 64).

Tools
Changing strings is easier with some tools at hand. First, a wire-cutter to cut your old strings. Second, a pair of pointed

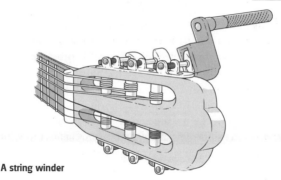

A string winder

pointed (*pincer-nosed*) pliers to help you get the ends of
the old strings out of the machine heads without cutting
your fingers. Thirdly, a *string winder* to speed up the loosening and tightening of the strings.

The whole set, or just one?

If one of your wound strings breaks, it's probably best to
replace the whole set (or at least all the wound ones), because unless the strings are quite new, a single replacement
will sound much brighter than the others and create an
unbalanced sound. If a plain string breaks, though, you can
usually replace just that one string; plain strings maintain
their sound for longer, so a new one doesn't stand out as
much. Luckily, wound strings happen to break less often.

One by one

When putting on a new set, it's best to replace the strings
one by one. If you remove them all at once, it will take the
guitar some time to readjust to the tension when you fit
the new ones, and this will temporarily affect the tuning.
Most guitarists start by changing either the low or high E.

Tuning as you go

Another advantage of changing the strings one by one is
that you can tune each new string to the one next to it –
assuming that the guitar is in tune in the first place.

Cleaning the fretboard

Some players like to remove all the strings at once, since it
allows them to give the fretboard and body a good clean.
But there's an alternative way – simply replace the strings
two at a time, cleaning underneath each pair as you go.

Elasticity

As strings lose their elasticity, they start to sound dull. The harder you play them, the faster this will happen, but even if you fit a set of strings and leave them untouched, they'll sound dull eventually. When they're brand new, however, strings are far too elastic, and when you put on a new set you have to tune them again and again. With steel strings it only takes a couple of hours to get past this stage, but with nylon strings, especially plain ones, it can take a day or two.

Pre-stretching

A good way to get rid of the extra elasticity more quickly is to slide a finger along the underneath of the strings, one by one, whilst carefully pulling them upwards, away from the guitar's body – then retune. Repeat this process until the tuning becomes more stable. Some classical players tune all the strings one semitone/half-step higher than they should be when they fit a new set, and then leave them overnight to lose the extra stretch on their own. This way the strings are absolutely new but not too elastic when you come to play them the next day.

On the table

You can change the strings with your guitar on your lap, but it's easier if you put it flat on a table. A towel or a piece of foam plastic underneath prevents scratches and keeps the guitar from sliding away.

CHANGING NYLON STRINGS

Fitting new strings isn't really that difficult – especially once you've done it a couple of times. Start by loosening the first string, until it's totally slack (a string winder will save you a lot of time). Then cut it in two places: close to the bridge, and just behind the nut, near the machine head. This way you are left with two short ends that are easier and safer to remove than an entire string.

At the bridge

Next you need to tie the new string around the bridge. The diagram opposite shows you how – the first step is shown with the first string (the high E), the second step is shown with the second string, and so on.

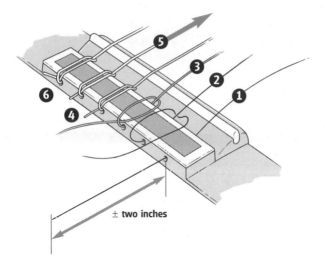

± two inches

1. Feed the string over the saddle and through the appropriate hole in the bridge, until about two inches stick out.
2. Pull this end back over the bridge and feed it under the string.
3. Thread the end through the loop. For wound strings just once will do, but many players feed plain strings through the loop three or four times (see the picture below).
4. The last 'knot' should always be behind the bridge, not on top of it.
5. Pull the string gently to tighten the knot.
6. Once the string is tuned, this is what it should look like at the bridge.

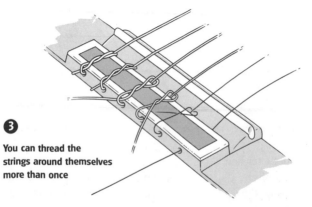

❸

You can thread the strings around themselves more than once

At the machine head

A similar knot should be tied at the machine head. To prevent slipping, when you tie the knot you should aim to leave enough slack in the plain strings so that once you've tuned them, they are wound around the posts three or four times; for wound strings three times is fine. Here's what to do:

1. Feed the string through the hole in the post. Try to leave enough slack in the string to make for the right number of windings.
2. Make a loop, as shown.
3. Tighten the string in the direction of the arrow – the knot should start to look like this.
4. Once the string has been tightened a little more, this is what the knot should look like.

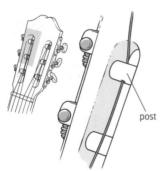

post

1. Through the hole

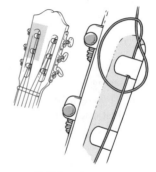

2. Make a loop

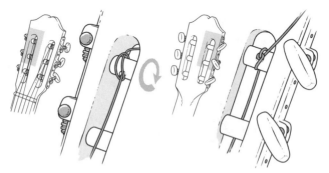

3. The right winding direction of the post　　**4. The resulting knot**

A little tension

To prevent a string from slipping out of its knot at the bridge while you are winding the machine head, you should keep it under a little tension. When winding the string, pull it away from the fretboard with your other hand, using your index finger to feed it through its groove in the nut. This makes for even windings. The diagram on page 66 shows you exactly how.

Inwards and outwards

As the diagram shows, both E-strings usually wind outwards from the holes in the posts, while the other strings wind in the opposite direction, towards the middle of the head.

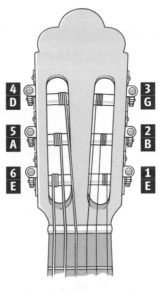

Extra length

Most strings are too long. If you knot them to the posts at their very ends, you may finish up with so many windings that they get stuck against the inside of the slot. The solution is to leave the string with just enough slack to make for the required number of windings. Cut off the excess when you've finished tuning.

The winding directions of the strings on the posts

Tips

- Loose ends at the bridge may buzz against the top, so cut them off.
- Long loose ends at the head can also buzz; it's best to cut them off about half an inch from the post.
- Instead of pulling a plain string through the loop at the bridge more than once, you can make a knot at the very end of the string. Thread the end with the knot through the loop just once, and make sure it ends up on the back of the bridge. Pull the string tight, and it's fixed.
- Some nylon strings come with *ball ends*. They have a little ball at one end to save you tying any sort of knot at the bridge – you just pull the string through the hole, starting at the back. However, most players prefer normal strings.

CHANGING STEEL STRINGS

Most steel-string guitars use pins to attach the strings to the bridge. Others come with slotted bridges, similar to the ones found on nylon-string guitars (see opposite). Steel strings need to be completely unwound before you remove them – cutting a string that still has any tension in it can be dangerous for both you and your guitar.

Steel strings are held in place by bridge pins

Cut and remove

Unwind the first string until it's totally slack (again, a string winder will save you time), and then cut it near the post and remove the leftover end. At the bridge, the string is usually attached with a bridge pin. String winders often have a special notch to remove these pins. As an alternative

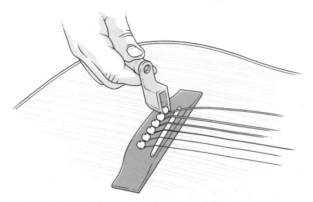

Many string winders have a notch for removing bridge pins

you can use a pair of wire cutters, or even a screwdriver – though you can easily damage an instrument with these tools, so you should be especially careful. When the pin is out, you can remove the string.

At the bridge

Insert the ball end of the new string into the hole. If there is a groove in the hole, let the string run through it. There should be grooves in the pins too – make sure that you insert each one the right way around, so that the string runs through the groove. Whilst inserting the pin, lightly pull the string over the saddle. Keep pulling the string while firmly (but not too firmly) pushing the pin into place.

Slotted bridges

If your guitar has a *slotted bridge*, just pull each string through its appropriate hole – the ball ends secure them, so you don't need to tie a knot. Many roundbacks come with slotted bridges, but they are also found on other types of guitars. A tip: be careful when you pull the strings through the bridge. Pulling too fast can wear down the wood, and the sharp ends of the strings can easily scratch the guitar or pierce your skin.

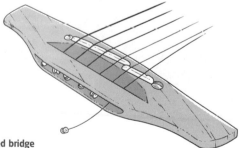

A slotted bridge

Too long

Just like nylon strings, most steel strings are too long. So, don't attach them to the machine heads right at their ends or you'll end up with too much string wound around each post. They are also like nylon strings in that by the time you've tuned them, the plain strings should be wrapped around the posts about three or four times, and wound strings about three times. You can cut off the excess of a string either when you've finished fitting and tuning it, or before you attach it to the post, leaving around 2 inches of slack for the windings.

At the machine head
First turn the post so that the hole faces the string.

1. Feed the string through the post. Try to leave enough slack in the string to make for the right number of windings.
2. Pass the string over and round the post once.

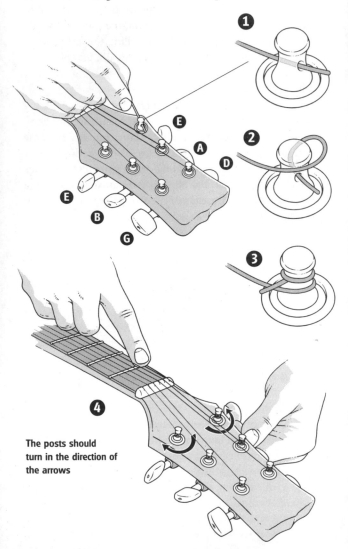

The posts should turn in the direction of the arrows

3. Start winding the machine head, making sure that the string now runs underneath the end which is sticking out of the hole.
4. Lift the string from the fretboard with your other hand, keeping it under a little tension. Use your index finger to guide it through the groove in the nut.

A better tone

The posts are shaped like hourglasses, so that they push the windings of each string together. If a string is the right length, then once it has been tuned, the windings should be packed together around the 'waist' of the post only.

Surprisingly, if this is the case, then you'll actually get a better tone, and your strings won't go out of tune as quickly.

String tips

• Don't get any **kinks** in your strings, because they can easily result in breakage. There's one exception to this rule – some players use a pair of pliers to make a small kink at the end of each string (after they've cut it to the right length), so that it hooks around the post.
• It may be hard to **tell an E-string from a B-string** once they're both out of their packets – so don't unpack a string until you're ready to put it on.
• Some manufacturers print **the names or the numbers** of each string on its packet. Others only print the gauges, usually in both inches and millimetres.
• Make sure you never tune your guitar **too high or too low**. If you tune it too high, you can snap strings and cause damage to your guitar; if it's too low the strings may rattle. Besides, a guitar sounds best when it's tuned to its proper pitch. More about tuning is explained in the next chapter.

9. TUNING

Each time you play your guitar, you have to tune up. Tuning isn't as hard as it may seem at first, though. You just need to know a few simple tricks, and learn how to listen in the right way. Read on...

The six guitar strings are tuned to the following pitches:

String ①	**E**	(the thinnest, highest string)
String ②	**B**	
String ③	**G**	
String ④	**D**	
String ⑤	**A**	
String ⑥	**E**	(the thickest, lowest string)

Eating And Drinking

As mentioned in chapter two, a good memory aid for these pitches is: Eating And Drinking Gives Brain Energy.

Playing on your own

When you play on your own, your strings have to be in tune with each other, but they don't necessarily have to be exactly E, A, D, G, B and E. If they're a long way off, though, they can cause you a whole number of problems.

Too low, too high

If the overall tuning is too low, your guitar might still sound in tune, but the strings

EADGBE
6 5 4 3 2 1

may rattle against the frets. Also, they'll be looser so you may accidentally bend them a little, causing you to play out of tune. If the strings are tuned too high, they're more likely to snap, the guitar will be harder to play and you may even bend the neck.

Playing with others

When playing with others, all the instruments must, of course, be in tune with each other. If you're playing with a piano, or any other instrument that cannot be tuned by the player, then you need to tune to that, but at other times you may have to tune to any other instrument, an electronic tuner, a metronome or a tuning fork.

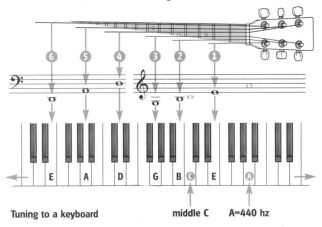

Tuning to a keyboard   middle C   A=440 hz

Tuning forks

A *tuning fork* is a small, two-pronged metal fork that produces a note for you to tune to. You tap it against your knee and then either hold it near your ear or touch the base of it to the bridge of your guitar to hear the note. Most tuning forks produce the note A, because that's the note that most classical musicians tune to, but you can also get ones that produce the note of the guitar's open high E-string. The best way to tune to an 'A' tuning fork is discussed later in this chapter – for now, we'll concentrate on the E.

A tuning fork

Tuning the high E-string

It's possible to tune a guitar to any note, but it's easiest to tune to one of the notes of the open strings. Once you have one string in tune, you can tune all the others from it. If you're tuning to a piano, a keyboard, another guitar or an 'E' tuning fork, then you can tune your high E-string first. Here's what to do:

- If you're using a piano or keyboard, the note that you need is the E to the right of 'middle-C', which lies at the middle of the keyboard.
- Play your reference note and listen to it for a few seconds.
- Play your open E-string, and try to hear whether the note sounds higher or lower.
- If the guitar's note sounds lower, tighten the string slightly.
- If the guitar's note sounds higher, first loosen the string until it sounds too low, and then slowly tighten it from there.
- Keep comparing and altering until the two notes sound exactly the same.

Two tips

When you're a beginner, it may be hard to hear if a string sounds too high or too low. A helpful technique is to sing the pitches that you hear – you'll soon learn how to 'feel' which one is higher. Another tip: whenever a string sounds too high, loosen it until it sounds too low, and then go up from there. This way, it's easier to hear what you're doing and the strings stay in tune for longer.

The other strings

Once the high E-string is in tune, you can tune the others to it. Basically, all you have to do is tune each string to the one next to it. So, first you tune the B to the high E; then you tune the G to the B, the D to the G, and so on. This is known as *relative tuning*. The following diagram and instructions explain what to do.

Fretboard diagrams

When a guitar is properly tuned, playing the B-string at the fifth fret creates the same note as playing the high E-string open. This is shown in the first fretboard diagram, and the similar relationships between the other strings are shown in the other four diagrams. Here's how they work:

- The numbers of the strings are shown at the bottom.
- The names of the strings are shown at the top.
- The black dot shows you where to fret the strings.
- The small circle underneath shows you which open string the fretted note should sound the same as.
- The letters at the very top show you which two strings each diagram deals with, and the note that you should hear when you're comparing them.

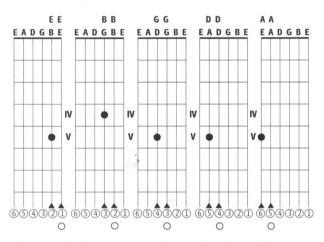

The black dots show you where to fret the string; the small circle underneath shows you which open string the fretted note should sound the same as.

Tuning the B to the E

Play the high E-string (that you just tuned) and listen to the note for a few seconds. Then play the B-string at the fifth fret, as shown on the diagram. If the B-string sounds too low, carefully tighten it. If it sounds too high, first loosen it until it sounds too low, and then slowly tighten it up from there.

And so on...

Now, continue to tune the other strings in the same way, as shown in the diagrams. Notice that you use the fifth fret (indicated by V) to tune all of the strings, except when you tune the third one (G) to the second (B). Here, you use the fourth fret (indicated by IV).

Starting with the low E

If you're playing alone, you don't always need a reference pitch – especially if your guitar is still nearly in tune from the last time you played. In this case, it's best to start with the low E, because it's the heaviest string and therefore generally stays in tune the best. So, first you tune the A to the low E, then the D to the A, the G to the D, and so on – tuning the open string to the fretted note each time. It's worth remembering, though, that even the low E drops in pitch, so do check your tuning against another instrument, a tuning fork or an electronic tuner (page 75–76) from time to time.

Starting with the A-string

Sometimes you may have to tune with an A as your reference pitch, because this is a standard tuning note for all instrumentalists. However, the particular A which most musicians use is the one that you play on a guitar on the fifth fret of the high E-string – two octaves higher than the open A-string. This note is known technically as the '440 hertz A', because it is made up of exactly 440 vibrations per second. It is the note of most tuning forks, and lots of electronic metronomes can also produce it.

Three options

When you tune to the 440 Hz A, you have three options:
- First, you can tune the open A-string to the reference A (not ideal because the open string is two octaves lower).
- Second, you can tune the high E-string, played at the fifth fret, to the reference A (not ideal because you have to use both hands).
- Third, and by far the best way, is to tune the fifth fret harmonic of the A-string to the reference A. This is explained in the following section.

HARMONICS

Using harmonics (see page 32) may make your tuning both faster and more accurate. The harmonics that you use for tuning are those above the fifth and seventh frets. To hear them really well, touch the string very lightly at the appropriate place with a left-hand finger, and then strike the string firmly, and close to the bridge, with your right hand.

Why use harmonics?

Tuning with harmonics has numerous advantages. First, the note of a harmonic keeps on sounding even when you've removed your left hand from the string, so you can tune the note whilst actually listening to it. Second, there's a good method to help you hear when the strings are exactly in tune. When the two harmonics that you're using to tune a string are almost the same and played simultaneously, you hear a wavy rhythm. When you hear this, carefully tighten or loosen the string that you're tuning. The closer you get, the slower the rhythm becomes. When the waves disappear, the two strings are in tune with each other. If the rhythm speeds up again, then you've gone too far.

Harmonics diagrams

These diagrams work in exactly the same way as those on page 71, except now the black dots indicate where you should lightly touch the strings to create harmonics.

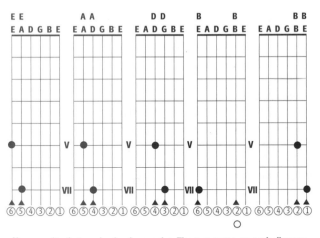

How a guitar is tuned using harmonics. The two notes on each diagram should sound exactly the same.

In all except one of the diagrams there are two harmonics, which you should tune to sound exactly the same. As the fourth diagram shows, when you come to tune the B-string, you have to play it open and compare it with the seventh fret harmonic of the low E. (You can use the twelfth fret harmonic of the B-string, instead of playing it open, but this raises the pitch by one octave.)

The 440 Hz A

Playing the harmonic at the fifth fret of the A-string produces the 440 Hz A that is often used for tuning. This is the best way to tune to the A.

Twelve-string guitars

A twelve-string guitar has the six normal guitar strings, but each one has a partner string. For both the high E and the B, the extra string is simply an exact repeat, but for the G, D, A and low E, the accompanying string is thinner and sounds one octave higher. The thinner of the two G's is the highest sounding guitar string – even higher than the high E.

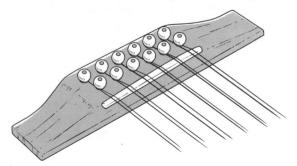

The bridge of a twelve-string guitar

Acoustic bass guitars

The four strings of an acoustic bass guitar are tuned the same as the four lowest strings on a regular guitar (E, A, D, G) – but one octave lower.

Guitar tuning tips

• A set of **pitch pipes** is a cheap, small alternative, to a tuning fork or an electronic tuner. They have the advantage of giving you the note of each string, but they often slip out of tune themselves, so a tuning fork is a better investment.

• You can, of course, tune each string to the appropriate note of a keyboard instrument. If it's an electronic one, use an **even sound without any effects**. A tip: always check the resulting tuning by using one of the relative tuning methods described above.

• **Strings detune faster** when brand new (be patient, or pre-stretch them – see page 60) or when they slip (put them on properly – see chapter 8).

- If the **nut's grooves** aren't wide enough for the strings you're using, tuning may be difficult and uneven. A temporary solution is to press the string behind the nut while you're tuning it (tune, press, listen, tune, press, etc). A better solution is to have the nut replaced or adjusted.

- Tuning can be made even smoother if you sprinkle some **graphite** (available at most hardware stores) into the grooves of the nut, or rub them with a pencil point.

Intervals

An *interval* is the difference in pitch between two notes. Some players like to tune up by listening to the intervals between the strings, without fretting them or playing harmonics. The A-string is supposed to sound a *perfect fourth* (five semitones/half-steps) higher than the low E-string. A perfect fourth is what you hear when you sing the first two syllables of *Amazing Grace, Here Comes the Bride* or *Oh, Christmas Tree*. Sing the first syllable at the pitch that the low E-string gives you, then tune the A-string to the pitch of the second syllable.

Oh When the Saints

The same interval is used when going from strings A to D, D to G, and B to high E. The only exception is going from G to B – the interval between these strings is a *major third* (four semitones/half-steps). When tuning the B to the G, you can use the first two syllables of *Oh When the Saints Go Marching In.*

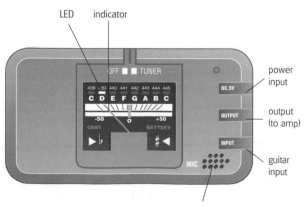

A chromatic electronic tuner indicates which tone it 'hears'

Electronic tuners

Yet another way to tune your guitar is to use an *electronic tuner*, or *tuner*. These devices 'hear' the note you're playing, and tell you whether it's in tune, too high, or too low. On some models you have to set a dial to tell the tuner which string you're tuning. *Chromatic tuners*, which are usually more expensive, actually recognize the pitch you're playing and indicate it on the display. On either type, there are usually two arrows, which tell you whether you should tune up or down to get the exact pitch. For an acoustic guitar you need a tuner with a built-in microphone – most of them have one.

Tips

• After you've tuned with an electronic tuner, check your tuning with one of the methods described above.

• If a sharp sign (♯) lights up on a chromatic tuner, it means you're playing a note that's one semitone/half-step higher than the name of the note indicated. For example, if a D and a ♯ light up, you're playing a D♯, and you need to tune down to get to a D.

• The flat sign (♭) indicates that a note is one semitone/half-step lower.

ALTERNATIVE TUNINGS

There are various ways to tune a guitar other than E, A, D, G, B, E. The most popular alternative is to use an *open tuning*, which means that the notes of the open strings form a particular chord. A common example is D, G, D, G, B, D (from low to high). This is known as *G major tuning* because strumming all the open strings together creates a G major chord (a chord made up of the notes G, B and D). With an open tuning you can play many chords, and often whole songs, just by placing your left-hand index finger over all six strings (this is called a *barré*) and sliding it from fret to fret.

Slides

Open tunings work particularly well with a *slide*. A slide is a tube, usually made out of metal – which you put on one of your left-hand fingers and 'slide' over the strings. They are especially popular with country and blues players. The term *bottleneck* is also used, because the first slide players actually used bottlenecks – and glass slides are still available today.

Fingerpicking
G major tuning is often used by fingerpickers as well as slide players. Fingerpickers also favour D, A, D, G, A, D (known as 'Dadgad' or *D tuning*), which was first used by English folk guitarists.

Personal tunings
Some guitarists use their own personal tunings. For example, E, A, C#, E, A, E (*A major tuning*), was made famous by Bonnie Raitt. King Crimson's Robert Fripp developed the C, G, D, A, E, G tuning, although he kept it secret for a long time.

Capos
The guitar is one of the few instruments on which you can play a piece of music at different pitches (in a different *key*) without changing what your fingers have to do. All you need is a *capo* (see page 37), which you mount just behind any fret on the neck, to raise the overall tuning of the guitar. This is especially useful for playing with singers (including yourself) because it makes it easier to sing songs which otherwise would be too high or too low.

Slightly higher or lower
Occasionally a tuning which is slightly higher or lower than the standard one may be used, for instance with the A at 442 Hz, instead of 440 Hz. Such tunings are most commonly employed for playing with an instrument that cannot tune to the modern notes, like a very old flute. Many electronic tuners can be adapted to other tunings, and tuning forks are available in various versions of the note A.

10. PICKS AND NAILS

Steel-string, classical and flamenco guitarists, not to mention fingerpickers, all have a different way of striking the strings. Whether you should pluck, strum or pick your guitar depends on the style of music you play and the sort of sound you want to achieve.

There are many ways to change a guitar's sound – what strings you use, for example, and which bit of them you play (you get a bright, biting tone near to the bridge, and a stronger, warmer tone closer to the fretboard). Equally important, though, is what you use to strike the strings – a hard pick and a fleshy fingertip make for two very different sounds.

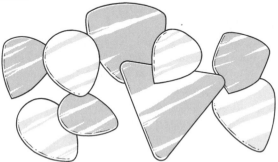

Picks come in all sorts of shapes, weights and sizes

PICKS

Picks, otherwise known as *plectrums*, are the small, flat triangular objects that most steel-string and electric guitarists use to strike the strings. They were originally carved out of bone or ivory, but are now almost always made of plastic. In general, playing with a pick gives a brighter, more penetrating tone than playing with the fingers. There are things that you can't play with a pick, but also things that you can't play without one.

The range

Most music shops offer a wide variety of picks, in all different shapes, weights, sizes and colours. Brightly coloured ones are easier to find if you drop them, but for the rest your choice depends on how you play, the sound you want, and what feels most comfortable.

Heavy and light

Each brand produces various weights of pick. A light one may be as thin as 1/64" (less than 0.5mm), but a heavy one can be more than twice as thick. Thicker picks make for a heavy, full-bodied sound – they both require and provide more precision.

Hard or soft

Generally, a thick plectrum is less bendy than a thin one. However, different picks are made of different types of plastic, so you can get thick ones that are flexible and thin ones that are hard. The only way to find out what suits you best is to try a selection – they're very cheap. If you want a really hard pick, try to find a metal one.

Which pick?

For chord playing most guitarists prefer quite thin picks, because they're easy to use and make for an even sound. Solo guitarists often go for smaller, harder ones. If you get sweaty fingers, try a pick with a non-slip surface, or one with a rubber or cork grip.

Fingers and thumbs

Playing with *fingerpicks* and *thumbpicks*, as many finger-pickers do, is like a having a plectrum on each finger (see picture overleaf).

Brands

Some well-known pick brands are Jim Dunlop, Fender, Gibson, Herco, Ibanez and Schaller.

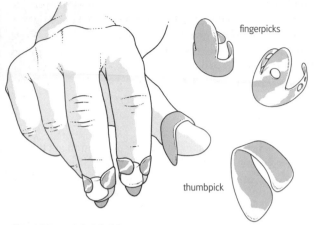

CHAPTER 10

Fingerpicks and thumbpicks

Pick tips

• Check picks for **rough edges**, which can quickly wear down your strings. A rough edge can usually be smoothened with some fine sandpaper or a nail file.

• If you want to use a pick, but your guitar has no **pickguard**, you might consider having one put on, to prevent the top from being scratched. It's better to go for a thin one, since a thick one can dull a guitar's sound. If you don't like the look of a pickguard, you can get a clear one – they're almost invisible.

NAILS

Flamenco guitarists mainly use their fingernails to strike the strings, which in part explains the biting sound that they create. Classical guitarists, and some fingerpickers, use both their nails and their fingertips. If you want to play with your nails, they have to be smooth, the right length and the right shape. Here are some tips.

Length and shape

The nail length and shape that will work best for you depends on many factors, including your playing style, the sound you want, and the hardness and thickness of your nails. Ask your teacher and other players for advice, but, once again, the only way to find the best solution is to experiment for yourself.

Nail files

A *nail file* is the best way to smooth and shape your nails. Lots of players use three- or four-way nail files, which are available at chemists/drugstores, and some guitar shops, usually costing around £5/$7. They have several different textures – you start off by using the coarsest section, then use the finer ones, and finish off by polishing your nail tips to a high gloss.

Soapy water

Water makes your nails go soft – especially hot, soapy water. Try to wear rubber gloves when you do the dishes or clean your car.

Nail strengthener

If your nails tear and peel easily, you could try using *nail strengthener*, which is sold at most chemists/drugstores. Apply it as directed on the bottle (usually every couple of weeks), until your nails are as hard as you want them to be. From then on, just use as much as you need to keep them that way. If your nails get too hard, they can break easily, so you should use strengtheners and similar products in moderation.

Personal remedies

Many players have their own remedies for weak nails. Some combine nail strengthener with nail oil, while others swear that nail strengthener is useless, and rub laurel balm or olive oil into their cuticles once a day. Some flamenco players even use superglue on their nail tips – a practice that can cause problems and should be used with a lot of caution. Consult your teacher, other players or a pharmacist if you want to know more.

Artificial nails

If nail strengtheners and other solutions don't work for you, then you might consider using artificial nails. They're not designed for guitar playing, and not all of them are suitable. A tip: if you're using artificial nails for guitar playing, they should very closely follow the shape of your own nails. Some players even make their own artificial nails, exactly in the shape they need.

11. MAINTENANCE AND CLEANING

It's important to keep your guitar in good condition –
both at home and on the road. Some jobs need to be
left to the specialists, but there is lots that you can do to
keep your guitar clean, and to prevent serious problems
from arising. This chapter is full of tips on maintenance,
cleaning, cases and insurance.

For serious problems, such as a crack in the top, a loose
brace or bridge, or a rattle you can hear but can't find, it's
best to go and see an expert. You may also consider using
a specialist to have your guitar 'set up'.

Setting up the action
Setting up a guitar is to fine-tune the action and the
intonation. If you change from heavy to light strings, or
vice versa, you may find that the action changes due to the
different levels of tension that the strings exert. If this
happens, or if you aren't happy with the action for any
other reason, you can have it adjusted. A specialist can set
the action by altering or replacing the saddle and/or the
nut. For a steel-string guitar, they can adjust the truss rod
too, which also influences the action.

CLEANING
A clean guitar is better to look at, easier to play and easier to
sell. Every player has their own cleaning techniques, but
here are some good tips.

Strings

Cleaning strings has been dealt with in chapter 8. Note that guitar cleaners that are good for the varnish may well be disastrous for the strings.

The fretboard

When wiping your strings after playing, you can easily clean the fretboard too, as described on page 59. If you do this regularly, you probably won't ever need to use a special fretboard cleaner. However, many players treat their fretboard to *fingerboard oil* or *fretboard conditioner* once or twice a year, just to keep it smooth and clean. An old, not too hard, toothbrush is good for cleaning down the edges of the frets and the nut.

Heavy grime

Some guitarists use steel wool, or kitchen and bathroom cleaners, on really dirty fingerboards. These experiments, though, are never without risk. Steel wool, for one, is likely to damage more than it cleans, and kitchen or bathroom products may be too abrasive or leave residues. The best way to find out exactly what you should or shouldn't use on your fretboard (and the rest of your guitar) is to ask a repairer. And think about bringing along your guitar when you do – then you could also choose to have it cleaned professionally.

The body

Cleaning the body is mainly a matter of lightly wiping it with a dry or slightly moist lint-free cloth on a regular basis. As mentioned before, an old T-shirt is good, but don't use a printed one since it might cause scratching.

Varnish

If you want to give the body a thorough clean, remove fingerprints and stains, or restore the finish to its original lustre, then use a proper guitar cleaner. Note that special finishes may require special cleaners – what's good for one finish might damage another. Bodies that are finished with oil or wax, for example, require particular types of cleaners. Once again, when in doubt, ask a specialist for advice, and consider taking your guitar along with you.

Special cleaners

Special guitar cleaners, with names such as *guitar polish*, *guitar juice* or *guitar gloss*, work well on most instruments. Some are just meant for cleaning the woodwork, while others are also supposed to restore the original lustre. Make sure that you read the instructions before choosing or applying such products.

Furniture polish

Some guitarists (including experienced ones) happily use normal household furniture polish on their guitars. Others warn against it, claiming that over time these polishes can cause the build up of a greasy residue on the instrument's surface. Special guitar cleaners (at least theoretically) don't have that effect. It's true that guitar cleaners cost a lot more, but they last a long time, so it's worth considering whether you'd actually save that much by using household products.

Brands

Guitar cleaners are supplied by companies such as D'Andrea, Dunlop, Number One, GHS and Kyser. Some guitar manufacturers, such as Gibson, Martin and Washburn, produce their own cleaners.

Machine heads

Open machine heads can be lubricated with light machine oil. You only need to apply a very tiny drop, and only once or twice a year. A good technique is to use a match as an applicator – dip it in the oil and then touch it on the machine head. Turn the tuner a couple of times, and the job's done. Alternatively, you could use a silicone-based slot spray; again, a tiny bit will do for months. Most enclosed machine heads are self-lubricating.

Dust

A small brush or a toothbrush (as mentioned earlier) can come in handy for removing dust and dirt from the corners and crevices. Some players use a vacuum cleaner, with its smallest head attachment, to remove dust from inside the body. It's easiest to do this when you're changing the strings, when the soundhole is more accessible.

AIR CONDITIONS

Wood can expand in high humidity and shrink in dry conditions. Sudden humidity changes and very dry air are both extremely bad for guitars. If a guitar gets too dry, the braces or the bridge may come loose, the top may crack, and frets (which don't shrink) can jut out from the sides of the neck (which does shrink). These are just some of the potential problems – so do take care.

Towels and humidifiers

Central heating and air conditioning are two of the main causes of dry air, so you should take extra care if you use either. Special guitar humidifiers, which you put in the soundhole when you're not playing, are a good way to protect your instrument. You can raise the level of humidity in a whole room by hanging wet towels, or water reservoirs, on your radiators. An electric humidifier, which you can buy at most department stores, is a more luxurious alternative.

Hygrometers

Guitars like about the same amount of air humidity as people – around 50–60%. Air humidity can be measured with a *hygrometer*, which can be bought at most department stores, and some music stores, for around £10/$15.

In the case

If you have to subject your guitar to an extreme change in temperature or air humidity (such as taking it from a cold, damp car to a hot, dry room), try to leave it in its case for a while, to let it get used to the new conditions slowly. Fifteen minutes is usually enough time, but the longer you leave it, the better it is for the instrument.

Heaters and windows

Try not to put your guitar anywhere that gets too hot or too cold, such as in direct sunlight, or near heaters, fireplaces or windows. If you want to hang it on a wall, an inside wall is preferable. This may sound over-cautious, but some luthiers claim that around ninety percent of all guitar problems are related to air humidity and temperature.

Solid tops

Guitars with solid tops are more sensitive to all of the above problems than those with laminated tops, but you should take care of any guitar.

CASES

Guitars are surprisingly fragile instruments, and if there is one accessory that your guitar should have, it's a case. You can pick one up with no padding for as little as £7/$10, but at this price it will probably offer very little protection.

Gig bags

Gig bags are soft cases with a protective inner lining. They cost around £15–35/$25–50, depending on the level of protection they provide. Most come with either one or two adjustable shoulder straps, and some have outside pockets, which are handy for stashing strings, music, picks, or even a music stand. If you're buying a gig bag, make sure that the zip is sturdy and well covered on the inside, so that it doesn't scratch your guitar.

Hard cases

Hard cases, or *hard-shell cases*, offer much better protection than gig bags. You should make sure, though, that the case fits your guitar perfectly – a badly fitting case can cause serious problems such as a bent neck. Avoid cases that are too big, as guitars bang around inside them.

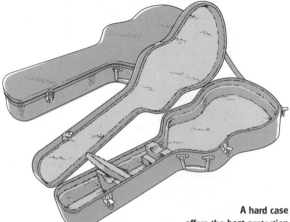

A hard case offers the best protection

ON THE ROAD

If you're taking your guitar on the road, you should be extra careful. Here are a few tips:

- If your guitar has a **serial number**, you'll probably find it on the back of the head or on the label in the body, but occasionally it is somewhere else on the instrument. Jot the number down, in case the guitar is ever stolen or lost. (There's a form to do this on p.118)

- Consider **insuring** your guitar. Your home contents insurance may cover your guitar (depending on its value) against theft from, or damage due to fire in, the home. However, musical instruments usually fall under the 'valuables' insurance category, which means that you have to notify the company when you buy or acquire a guitar, and sometimes have to pay more. If you want your guitar to be covered against accidental damage, or when it isn't in the home, you usually have to extend your policy – and this is sometimes surprisingly expensive. Another option is to take out a totally separate policy for your instrument and equipment.

- Carry **spare strings** and **picks** in your guitar case. If your guitar has a pickup then also try to have one or two **extra leads/cords**, as well as a spare **battery** (see chapter 6), with you for gigs and practices.

- A **guitar stand** is handy for when you take a break from playing, or if you want to use more than one guitar in a gig. There are a wide variety of models available, some of which are specifically designed to fold away very small, and others that are designed more for sturdiness.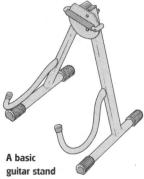

- Try not to leave your equipment in a **parked car** – and if you do have to, make sure that it's out of sight. Never leave a guitar on the back shelf, where it can be both clearly

A basic guitar stand

seen and exposed to direct sunlight. When you're **driving**, keep your guitar on the back seat, which doesn't get as cold (or as hot) as the boot/trunk.

- If you're **flying** with your guitar, it's best to carry it as hand luggage. Most airlines allow this.

12. BACK IN TIME

Stringed instruments have been around for millennia – and the guitar has ancestors dating back to the ancient Greek lyre played in myth by Orpheus. The modern acoustic guitar's more immediate parentage lies with the medieval lute, the Moorish guitar, the Arabic *oud*, and in particular the Spanish guitars of the nineteenth and twentieth centuries.

A seventeenth-century guitar with five double strings

The lute was the most popular stringed instrument in Renaissance Europe and its legacy in guitar manufacture remains in the term for guitar makers – *luthiers*.

However, the first instruments that resembled today's guitar emerged in the sixteenth century; they generally had five single or double strings, lacking a low E.

Antonio de Torres Jurado

Some time between 1850 and 1860 the Spaniard Antonio de Torres Jurado built an instrument close to today's classical guitar. Torres combined a slightly bigger body with an improved bracing pattern (fan-bracing) and the current scale – which turned out to be a fantastic recipe. Though his name is still around, Torres never really profited from his valuable contributions to the history of the guitar; poverty even forced him to accept other kinds of jobs from time to time.

Before nylon

Classical or Spanish guitars have only been referred to as 'nylon-string guitars' for around fifty years – that's as old as nylon strings are. Before that time gut was used for the plain strings, while the wound strings had a silk core. Nylon strings took over from gut quite easily as they sound brighter and louder, they're easier to play, they're more reliable and consistent, and their tuning doesn't drop when air humidity goes up.

THE STEEL-STRING GUITAR

While Torres was working on the classical guitar in Spain, Christian Friedrich Martin was designing the forerunner of today's steel-string guitar in the US.

Martin and the Dreadnought

The German luthier Martin (1796–1867) moved to America in the 1830s, settling in Pennsylvania. There, he introduced the technique of X-bracing, which is still used on most steel-string guitars today. This proved a vital development when high tension steel strings were introduced in the late nineteenth century. The big steel-string guitar known as the *Dreadnought* was first made by the Martin company in 1916.

Archtops

In the 1930s, archtop guitars, predominantly used by jazz players, became increasingly popular. The archtop doesn't

An archtop with a pickup

seem to have had a single inventor, though the name of luthier Orville Gibson, founder of the Gibson company, is often mentioned. The electric archtop or semi-acoustic guitar is still favoured by many jazz guitarists.

Folk and unplugged

The flattop steel-string guitar was the key instrument of European and American folk music – and sold in huge numbers during the folk music boom of the 1950s and 1960s. More recently, it received a boost through MTV's *Unplugged* sessions.

Electro-acoustic

The electro-acoustic guitar became popular in the 1980s, Ovation being the first major company to manufacture acoustic guitars with built-in piezo pickups.

13. THE GUITAR FAMILY

The modern acoustic guitar is related to every other instrument that makes its sound with strings, such as the piano, the harp and the violin. This chapter only deals with close relatives – the guitar family – which includes the flamenco, the doubleneck, the cuarto and, of course, the electric guitar.

Guitars are made in many different ways, by many different people and in many different countries, so there's often quite a lot of confusion about which guitars are called what. The following pages should clarify things a little, but bear in mind that none of the terms introduced here are unambiguous – many are used by a number of different companies to describe various different things.

Dreadnoughts and Jumbos

Chapter 5 introduced the two best-known models of steel-string guitar – the Dreadnought and the Jumbo. These were originally specific designs, by Martin and Gibson respectively, but now many manufacturers produce 'Dreadnought' or 'Jumbo' models. Such guitars often have a D or a J in the model name or number.

Other models

Another well-known design by Martin is the narrow-waisted *000* (pronounced 'triple-oh'), also known as the *Auditorium*. A *Grand Auditorium*, one size bigger, resembles a Jumbo but has a shallower body. The *Grand Concert*, or *00*, is one size smaller, and the *Concert* model, *0*, is smaller still. *OM* stands for *Orchestra Model*, which is basically a

000 with a longer scale. All these names are also used by other brands, but not always to describe exactly the same models.

Electric guitars

Most electric guitars have a solid body and two or three pickups. Such instruments are usually referred to as *solid bodied guitars*, but other names, such as *axes* are also sometimes used. (Want to know more? Read *The Rough Guide to Electric Guitar and Bass Guitar.*)

A well-known solid body guitar – the Fender Stratocaster, known as the 'Strat'

Hollow bodied guitars

Electric guitars without solid bodies are collectively known as *hollow bodied guitars*, *semi-acoustics* or *archtops*, and they're especially favoured by jazz players. Those with thick bodies, sometimes called *full bodied archtops*, look very similar to acoustic archtops (see page 89) but with one or two visible pickups. Guitars with shallower bodies, such as the famous Gibson ES-335, are often referred to as *slimlines* or *thinlines*. (Confusingly, the *Thinline* is also a type of pickup marketed by Martin.)

Flamenco guitars

The nylon-stringed flamenco guitar is very similar to the classical guitar, but usually has a slightly smaller body. The size and shape, as well as a thin top and the woods used, combine to give the instrument its penetrating tone. Some traditional flamenco guitars have wooden *tuning pegs*, similar to those of a violin, instead of machine heads. One or two pickguards (*golpeadores* in Spanish) protect the top.

Requinto and ukulele

The Spanish introduced the guitar into Central and South America in the sixteenth century, and since then many variations of the instrument have developed there. The *requinto* (see page 28), the five-string *quinto* and the four-string *cuarto* are some of the smaller sized, nylon-stringed examples. The *ukulele*, developed in Hawaii, has its roots in the Portuguese *machete*.

More strings

Twelve-string guitars have a set of double strings (see page 74), but you can also get guitars with more than 6 single strings. The most common type is the 7-string guitar, which has an extra bass string (tuned to the A below the low E), but 10- or even 11-string classical guitars also exist.

An electro-acoustic doubleneck (Ovation)

Doublenecks

Just about the only guitars with more than twelve strings are *doublenecks* – as used by the likes of Jimmy Page (Led Zeppelin) and Richie Sambora (Bon Jovi). These guitars usually have one 12-string neck and one 6-string neck, allowing the player to switch between the two. They are usually electric guitars, but you do come across quite a few acoustic doublenecks, which are often produced as special editions or for a custom order. Ovation is one of the few companies that produce electro-acoustic doublenecks.

Less strings

Apart from their hollow bodies, acoustic bass guitars are just like electric ones: they're tuned the same way and they're both available with either four or five strings, and with or

An acoustic bass (Taylor)

without frets. Most acoustic bass guitars come with a pickup, since their acoustic volume is rather limited.

Almost solid

Guitars with almost solid bodies are known as *semi-solids, shallow-bodied guitars* or *thinlines*. These instruments, which are available with either nylon or steel strings, aren't quite loud enough to use without an amp. A well-known example is the Gibson Chet Atkins Classic Electric – an electric, nylon-string guitar with a piezo pickup and a shallow body with two small sound chambers. Another example is the Godin Acousticaster, which is said to sound like an amplified acoustic guitar but play like an electric one. You can even get semi-solids with *MIDI functions*, which can be hooked up to computers, keyboards and other MIDI instruments.

The Acousticaster (Godin)

Travel guitars

The two most popular manufacturers of *travel guitars* are Martin and Taylor. Martin produce both steel- and nylon-string *Backpacker Guitars*, which have a scale length of 24" (only slightly shorter than a regular guitar) but a tiny little body. The *Baby Taylor*, a three-quarter-size steel-string guitar with a scale length of just under 23", looks much more like a regular instrument.

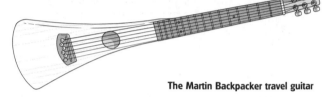

The Martin Backpacker travel guitar

Parlor guitars

Another type of small guitar is the *Parlor* guitar, which was very popular at the end of the nineteenth century, especially among female players. It's tuned to the notes G, C, F, B♭, D, G – a minor third (three semitones/half-steps) higher than a regular guitar.

Resonator guitars

Before the advent of amplifiers, the only way for a guitarist to get a bit more volume was to use a *resonator guitar*. Developed in America in the 1920s, these guitars usually have a metal body and a top that contains one or more discs which vibrate and amplify the sound. Resonator guitars produce a very metallic tone and are mainly used by blues players. They are also known as *Dobros*, because they were first produced by the Dobro company, which was run by Ed and Rudy Dopyera – the **Do**pyera **Bro**thers. Dobro is still the best-known manufacturer of resonator guitars, but other brands such as National are also popular. Four-string basses and electro-acoustic versions are available as well as the standard six-string models.

A resonator guitar

Banjo

The *banjo*, widely used in bluegrass and a variety of other styles of music, is a four- or five-string fretted instrument with a drumhead for a top. Banjos are usually played with fingerpicks.

14. HOW THEY'RE MADE

If you want to know a bit more about acoustic guitars, it's good to have an idea of how they're made. Guitar construction is an extremely complicated process, but this chapter outlines some of the basic principles.

A master luthier may only make one instrument every few months, while a factory with around twenty employees can knock out up to twenty thousand guitars every year. The luthier will carefully select the wooden parts to create the best possible sound, but much less care will be taken in the factory.

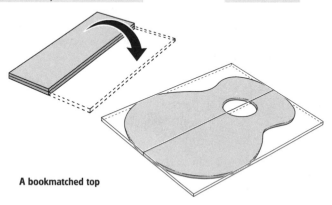

A bookmatched top

Bookmatched tops and backs

A *bookmatched* top is made by splitting a thin plank of solid wood in half. The two resulting pieces, which are the mirror image of each other, are then glued together. A laminated top is sometimes made to look like a solid top by using this method for the top ply.

The back

The back usually consists of two or three parts, and is often bookmatched like the top. However, it is made out of a different sort of wood, and is often decorated at the joins with a very thin, and often coloured, wooden strip.

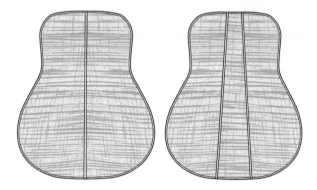

Bookmatched backs, in two and three parts

The sides

The two pieces of wood that make up the sides or rims of the guitar are soaked in water, bent using heat, and then clamped in a mould. On the inside, where the sides meet the top and back, *linings* (either with or without saw-cuts) are used to strengthen the join. Usually, the edges of the body, and sometimes also those of the head and neck, are finished with wooden or plastic binding.

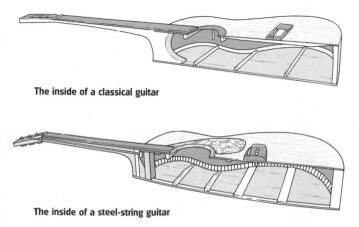

The inside of a classical guitar

The inside of a steel-string guitar

CHAPTER 14

A guitar mould

The neck, head and fretboard

The neck, head and fretboard often look like one solid piece of wood, but they're not. Necks are often made of mahogany, because it's tough and easy to work with, and doesn't warp easily. The fretboard is a separate piece of wood that's glued onto the neck.

Dovetail joints

On most steel-string guitars the neck is attached with a *dovetail joint*, and a similar method is used for classical guitars. Glue is usually used to hold everything in place, but some steel-string guitars also use screws.

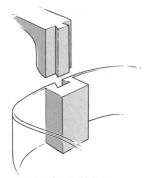

The dovetail joint of a steel-string guitar

Varnish and hardware

To finish a guitar, many thin coats of varnish are applied – often more than ten – and each is polished separately. After that the *hardware* (the nut, saddle, frets, machine heads, etc) is fitted, and then finally the strings are put on.

15. THE BRANDS

**There are thousands of guitar companies and luthiers –
just a list of their names would fill a book of this size. The
following chapter introduces some of the main brands,
and gives an idea of their price ranges and main products.**

Some guitar brands only produce high- or low-budget
instruments while others cover all price brackets.
Obviously, though, companies are permanently adding to
their price and product range, so the following information
is only intended to give you a rough idea of each company
mentioned.

Nylon and steel
Many non-Spanish manufacturers produce instruments
in the lower price ranges – both classicals and steel-strings
as well as electric and bass guitars. Some examples are
Aria, **Encore**, **Samick** (one of the world's biggest guitar
manufacturers) and **Vantage**. **Yamaha**, who also produce
countless other instruments and products, make guitars in
pretty much every style and for every budget.

CLASSICAL GUITARS
Most classical guitars are made in Spain, especially the
areas around Madrid (in the centre of the country) and
Valencia (on the east coast).

Spanish names
In the same way that many non-German companies
produce pianos with German names, guitars that aren't

made in Spain are often given Spanish names. Some companies, such as **Aria** (based in Japan), manufacture most of their products in the Far East but have their top-of-the-range classical guitars made in Spain.

Spanish beginners' models

It isn't only expensive guitars, though, that come out of Spain – some of the many Spanish brands that mainly produce instruments in the lowest price ranges are **Juan Salvador**, **Vincente Tatay Tomas**, **Maravilla**, **Ramon Torres**, **Triana** and **Prudencio Saez**. Brands like **Angel Lopez**, **Azahar** and **Manuel Serrano** also make more expensive guitars.

A wide range

Some companies produce guitars that sell for as little as £150/$200 but also produce those which cost five or ten times as much. Some examples are **Admira**, **Joan CashiMira**, **Cuenca**, **José Rodriguez**, **Manuel Rodriguez**, **Vincente Sanchis Badia** and **Alhambra** (whose guitars are made in one of Spain's largest factories, where both traditional and high-tech production methods are used). Alhambra, **José Ramirez** and **Esteve** are three of the 'classical' companies that also produce electro-acoustic guitars. **Amalio Burguet** guitars start at around £350/$500.

Concert guitars

A professional classical guitar, or concert guitar, usually costs upwards of £1500/$2000; some luthiers are so in demand that they have waiting lists of many years, and produce no guitars for less than £5000/$7000. Some of these specialists keep a very small workshop, but others run larger companies, building concert guitars themselves while overseeing the production of less expensive models. A few examples are introduced below.

Ramirez

José Ramirez started producing guitars in 1882, and since then members of the Ramirez family have taught their trade to countless other luthiers in the Madrid area. It is **José Ramirez IV** that currently runs the workshop. The student models, which start at around £500/$700, are made by other Spanish companies.

Other top luthiers

There are many excellent luthiers, but some of the best-known are **Manuel Rodriguez**, **Manuel Contreras** and **Conde Hermanos**. The latter produces a classical guitar model with a list price of over £7000/$10,000. **Paulino Bernabe** is another member of this select group, and has student models made under the name **Antonio Lopez**.

Japan

Perhaps surprisingly, Japan is home to quite a few very well-known 'Spanish guitar' luthiers. One example is **Asturias**, whose catalogue includes seven-, ten- and eleven-string guitars; **Kodairo** is a sub-brand of the Asturias company, and produces the less expensive models. **Kohno** makes concert guitars for £1500/$2000 and more. One of the longest established Japanese luthiers, **K. Yairi**, makes both classical and steel-string instruments.

STEEL-STRING GUITARS

The steel-string acoustic guitar was invented and developed in America, and some of the earliest brands, like Martin and Gibson, are still among the best. Most of the lower-priced instruments are made in Asia, especially in Korea – some of the biggest brands also produce classical guitars and have been mentioned above. In the same way that nylon-string guitars tend to be given Spanish names, most steel-string guitars get American names, regardless of where they're made. **Bloomfield** and **Bruce Wallace** are both good manufacturers of low-budget instruments.

The full range

Some examples of companies that produce guitars in the low, middle and high price ranges are **Bluebridge**, **Cort**, **Grant**, **Landola**, **Epiphone**, **Ibanez** and **Washburn** (the latter three are mainly known for their electric guitars).

Alvarez is a good example of how complicated the guitar industry can be: a Spanish-named brand, owned by an American company, that produce Korean-made steel-string guitars designed by the Japanese luthier Yairi...

Godin

The Canadian brand **Godin** has become especially famous

for its semi-solid electric guitars. **Simon & Patrick**, **Seagull** and **Norman** are three Godin sub-brands which make steel-string guitars that sell for around £350/$500 or more. A fourth Godin brand, **Art & Lutherie** produce low-budget guitars.

Fender and Gibson

The world's best-known manufacturers of electric guitars, **Fender** and **Gibson**, both also market acoustic guitars. Those from Gibson start at around £1500/$2000, while the Fender models are usually under £350/$500.

Expensive guitars

A number of companies concentrate on the higher price bracket, and their guitars can cost up to and above £7,000/ $10,000. **Martin**, **Taylor** and **Lowden** are three of the best-known high-budget brands.

Martin

The **Martin** company, founded in 1833, has played a very significant role in the development of the steel-string guitar. The current president, C. F. Martin IV, is a namesake and direct descendant of the founder.

Taylor

Expensive guitars are generally assumed to be totally hand-made, but this isn't always the case. High-quality **Taylor** guitars, as Bob Taylor proudly tells us, are constructed using computer-controlled machines at various stages of the production process.

Lowden

In Northern Ireland, George **Lowden** supervises the production of about a thousand guitars each year, including a number of nylon-string instruments. Lowden himself makes a limited number of guitars by hand.

Canadian guitars

Canada is the home of quite a few major guitar companies and luthiers, including Godin. Another major name is **Larrivee**, whose guitars cost around £1000–4000/ $1500–6000. **Morgan** and **Thompson** are former employees of Larrivee.

Smaller companies

As well as countless one-person workshops, where you can
have a guitar completely custom-made, there are many
small companies that concentrate on the high budget end
of the market. Examples of the latter are **Lakewood** and
Stevens in Germany, **Larkin** in Ireland, and **Guild**, **Tacoma**
and **Breedlove** (all founded by former Taylor employees)
in America. **RainSong**, based in Hawaii, make guitars out
of graphite. **Olsen**, **Santa Cruz**, **Dana Bourgouis**, **Goodall**
and **Collins** are some of the smaller companies that only
produce very expensive instruments.

ELECTRO-ACOUSTIC

Electro-acoustic guitars are produced by many companies,
but two brands which are particularly noted for such
instruments are Ovation and Takamine.

Ovation

Guitarist and helicopter manufacturer Charlie Kaman Sr.
created the first roundback guitars in 1966 and founded
the **Ovation** company, which is still by far the world's
biggest producer of roundbacks. American-made models
start at around £1000/$1500, but Kaman's company
produces less expensive instruments under the brand
name **Applause**.

Takamine

Takamine (Japanese for 'top of the mountain') was
founded in the 1960s and, unlike Ovation, produce electro-
acoustics that are based on traditional acoustic guitars.
Jasmine is the company's less expensive sub-brand.

GLOSSARY AND INDEX

This glossary briefly explains all the terms you will find in this book, and other guitar-speak words that you may come across as a player. The numbers refer to the page(s) that contain more information on each subject.

000, 00, 0 See: *Triple-0.*

10:1, 12:1, 14:1 *(38)* 10:1 machine heads offer faster but less precise tuning than 12:1 or 14:1 machine heads.

Abalone *(26)* Mother-of-pearl; product of a shellfish of the same name.

Acoustic amplifier *(49–50)* An amplifier that is specifically designed for use with acoustic instruments.

Acoustic guitar *(1)* A guitar that can be played without an amplifier. Originally, all guitars were acoustic, and so they were just called guitars. But the term 'acoustic guitars' is now used to distinguish such instruments from electric guitars.

Action *(36–37, 82)* The distance between the strings and the fretboard; also referred to as 'string height'. Action is also sometimes used to describe the feel of a guitar – a guitar which plays easily is said to have a 'good action'.

Amplifier See: *Acoustic amplifier.*

Archtop *(11, 90, 92)* A guitar with an arched top and (usually) two *f*-shaped soundholes. See also: *Flattop.*

Auditorium, Grand Auditorium *(91–92)* Steel-string guitar models.

Back *(7, 44, 97)* The back of a guitar's body.

Bass guitar, acoustic *(35–36, 39, 74, 94)* Most acoustic bass guitars have four strings, which are tuned one octave lower than the four lowest guitar strings.

Bass strings *(8)* The lower sounding (wound) strings of a guitar. See also: *Wound strings.*

Binding *(6, 7, 10)* An ornamental strip that runs around the edge of a guitar's body. Some guitars also have binding on the neck and head.

Body *(6, 10, 26–29, 31, 47, 97)* The hollow body of an acoustic guitar acts as a soundbox, amplifying the sound of the vibrating strings. Most electric guitars have solid bodies, which is why they sound much quieter when they're not plugged in.

Bookmatched top *(7, 96)* A bookmatched top is one where the left half is the mirror image of the right.

Bottleneck See: *Slide guitar.*

Bracing *(11–12, 43–44, 89)* The wooden struts that are glued to the underneath of the top, influencing the sound and reinforcing the wood. X-bracing is a very popular style for steel-string guitars, but horizontal, A- and V-bracing are also used. Most classical guitars have fan-bracing.

A-bracing

Bridge *(6, 9, 10, 11, 39)* The piece of wood glued onto the top, which the strings are attached to. The white strip on the bridge that the strings run over is the saddle. See also: *Saddle* and *Nut.*

Bridge pins *(10, 11, 64–65)* The pins that secure the strings of a steel-string guitar to the bridge.

Bridge saddle See: *Saddle.*

Camber See: *Radius.*

Capo *(37, 77)* A special clamp which you can mount on the neck of a guitar, changing the instrument's overall pitch. The name comes from the Italian 'capo d'astro'. If you capo the first fret, everything will sound one semitone/half-step higher, if you capo the second fret everything will sound two semitones/half-steps higher, and so on.

Cedar *(30)* A type of wood often used for the tops of classical guitars.

Classical guitar *(2–3, 5–9)* An acoustic guitar with nylon strings; also referred to as 'Spanish guitar' and 'nylon-string guitar'.

Compensated saddle See: *Saddle.*

Concert, Grand Concert *(91–92)* Steel-string guitar models.

Concert guitar, student guitars *(22–23, 100–101)* Classical guitar luthiers refer to their professional quality instruments as 'concert guitars', and their slightly less expensive models as 'student guitars' (although these can still cost well over £1000/ $1500). Conversely, some low-budget brands describe their cheapest models as concert guitars.

Custom Many luthiers will make 'custom guitars', to the exact specifications of the buyer. Some expensive brands offer 'custom options', such as a choice of various necks or tops.

Cutaway *(9, 28–29)* A section cut out from the body, to allow easier access to the higher frets.

Dobro See: *Resonator guitar.*

Dreadnought *(26–27, 89, 91)* A big, broad-waisted steel-string guitar.

Ebony *(31)* A hard, dark wood, often used for fretboards.

Electro-acoustic guitar *(13, 42, 46–49, 90, 103)* An acoustic guitar with a pickup and a pre-amp, which allow it to be hooked up directly to an amplifier.

Electronic tuner *(75, 76)* An electronic device which tells you whether a note is in tune; often shortened to 'tuner'.

Element See: *Pickup.*

Fan-bracing See: *Bracing.*

Feedback *(47–50)* A pickup sends the sound of a guitar to an amplifier, which then sends it to a speaker. Sometimes, the pickup 'picks up' its own sound from the speaker, and so sends the same sound back to the amplifier, which then sends it back to the speaker again. This goes round and round causing a loud piercing screech known as feedback. Amplified acoustic guitars are notorious for producing feedback. See also: *Notch filter*.

Fingerboard See: *Fretboard*.

Fingernails *(80–81)* Used to strike the strings by classical and flamenco guitarists, and some fingerpickers.

Fingerpicking *(27, 35, 77)* Steel-string guitar playing style; the right-hand thumb plays a bass line, while the fingers play a melody and accompaniment.

Fingerpicks *(79, 80)* Small plastic picks used for playing in the fingerpicking style. You attach one fingerpick to each finger, and a 'thumbpick' to your thumb.

Flageolet See: *Harmonic*.

Flamenco guitar *(30, 36, 80, 92)* Very similar to a classical guitar, but often slightly smaller. Flamenco guitars usually have thin tops, a cypress back, one or two pickguards *(golpeadores)* and quite a low action.

Flattop *(11, 90)* A term used to distinguish steel-string guitars with flat tops from those with arched tops. Classical guitars have flat tops, but the term isn't applied to them because there are no classical archtops. See also: *Archtop*.

Folk guitar See: *Steel-string guitar*.

Footstool A small, fold-up metal stool used by most classical guitarists. It is placed under the left foot to raise the height of the left leg and the guitar, creating a more comfortable playing position. Some players prefer to use a *knee cushion*, which sits between the left leg and the guitar, and serves the same purpose.

Fourteen-fret neck *(9, 32)* A guitar with a fourteen-fret neck is one where the neck meets the body underneath the fourteenth fret. A fourteen-fret neck does *not* only have fourteen frets (because the fretboard continues over the body). Most steel-string guitars have fourteen-fret necks. See also: *Twelve-fret neck*.

Fretboard *(6, 8, 10, 31–36, 83)* The front section of the neck which has the frets on, and which the strings run over; also known as the 'fingerboard'.

Frets *(6, 8, 10, 39, 42, 45, 57)* The metal strips that run across the fretboard.

Golpeador *(92)* Spanish for pickguard. See also: *Flamenco guitar.*

Grand Auditorium, Grand Concert *(91–92)* Steel-string guitar sizes.

Harmonic *(32–33, 72–74)* The tone you hear when striking a string that's not pressed down to a fret, but lightly touched at any one of certain specific points. For the strongest harmonics, these points are above the twelfth fret (the middle of the string), the seventh fret (a third of the string) and the fifth fret (a quarter of the string).
Harmonics are sometimes also called *overtones* or *flageolets.*

Head, headstock *(5, 10, 11, 97, 98)* The end of the neck, which houses the machine heads. Classical guitars have so-called 'slotted heads'. Another name for a head is 'peghead'.

Heel *(6, 7, 10)* The thick piece of wood where the neck joins the body.

Hygrometer *(85)* A device that indicates the level of air humidity.

Inlay *(22, 26)* Anything which is literally 'laid' into the wood. The markers, the binding and the decoration around the soundhole are often inlaid pieces of wood or other materials. See also: *Abalone.*

Insurance *(87).*

Intonation *(32–33, 43, 53)* On a guitar with bad intonation, the higher frets play out of tune with the lower frets. If the intonation is correct, the note that you get by playing a string at the twelfth fret should sound exactly one octave higher than the note of the open string.

Jumbo *(26–27, 91)* A large type of steel-string guitar, with a thin waist.

Knee cushion See: *Footstool.*

Laminated *(29–30, 44, 86)* A laminated top, back or side consists of a number of thin plys of wood glued together. See also: *Solid.*

Left-handed *(12–13)* Classical guitars can be quite easily adapted for left-handed players. If you want to play left-handed on a steel-string guitar, however, you'll need a 'left-handed guitar'.

Lower bout *(9, 10)* The lower, broader part of the body, also known as the 'belly'.

Luthier A guitar maker (from the term for a 'lute maker').

Machine heads *(6, 8, 10, 38, 42, 43, 84)* The devices on the head of a guitar, which the strings are attached to, and which are used to tighten and loosen the strings; also called 'tuners', 'tuning machines', 'tuning keys', 'tuning gears'. Classical guitars have open machine heads, but steel-string instruments usually have enclosed ones. The wooden versions on traditional flamenco guitars are called 'pegs', and this term is also sometimes used to describe modern machine heads.

Markers *(6, 8–10, 26, 32)* Dots or patterns on the fretboard which help you tell which fret is which.

Melody strings See: *Plain strings*.

Metronome *(19)* A small device that ticks or beeps

out a steady, adjustable pulse, helping you to work on your tempo and rhythm skills.

MIDI *(94)* Musical Instrument Digital Interface; an electronic system which allows certain musical instruments to be connected to each other and to computers. It is usually keyboards, digital pianos and synthesizers that feature MIDI, but MIDI guitars also exist. You could use a MIDI guitar to play the sounds of an electric piano, or even a drum machine.

Nails See: *Fingernails*.

Neck *(6, 7, 9, 10, 31–36, 98)* The section of a guitar that runs between the body and the head.

Notch filter *(47)* An electronic device that prevents feedback. See also: *Feedback*.

Nut *(6, 8–9, 10, 39–40, 75)* A small strip, usually made out of plastic, which the strings run over at the end of the fretboard. It keeps the strings at the correct distance from each other.

Open tuning *(76)* A way of tuning the guitar, so the notes of the six open strings form a chord, such as G major.

Overtone See: *Harmonic.*

Peg, peghead See: *Machine heads* and *Head.*

Pick *(78–80)* Also known as a plectrum; a small (usually triangular) piece of plastic, used for plucking the strings. Playing with a pick gives a more penetrating sound than playing with your fingers.

Pickguard *(9, 10, 26, 80, 92)* A thin plastic plate that protects a section of the top next to the strings, to stop the wood from being scratched by picks and nails. Pickguards aren't found on classical guitars.

Pickup *(13, 46–49, 87)* A device (a kind of transducer) which converts the vibrations of the guitar's strings into electrical signals. Electro-acoustic guitars usually come with a 'piezo pickup', which is located under the saddle. This type of pickup responds to both steel and nylon strings, unlike magnetic pickups, which only respond to metal strings. See also: *Electro-acoustic guitar.*

Plain strings *(8–9, 52–54, 58, 61, 62)* The thin, unwound strings; sometimes called 'melody strings' or 'trebles'. See also: *Wound strings.*

Plectrum See: *Pick.*

Posts, string posts *(6, 10, 51, 62–67)* The parts of the machine heads that the strings are actually attached to and wound around.

Pre-amp, pre-amplifier *(13, 46–47)* A device which amplifies the weak signal of a built-in pickup before sending it to an external amp. Most electro-acoustic guitars have built-in pre-amps.

Prices of guitars *(21–24, 47).*

Quarter-sawn *(44)* If a tree is sawn into segments, as shown in the picture opposite, you get so-called quarter-sawn wood, which allows for the production of thin yet strong tops. With this method, you get fewer tops out of each tree, so the wood is more expensive than *slab-cut* wood.

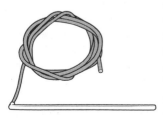

A piezo pickup

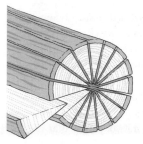

Quarter-sawn wood (top) is stronger that slab-cut wood

Radius *(34–35)* The curve of a fretboard; also known as 'camber'. On steel-string guitars, the fretboard is slightly rounded, being higher in the middle than at the edges. The degree of radius or camber is expressed in inches – the higher the number, the flatter the fretboard. Classical guitars have flat fretboards.

Requinto *(28, 93)* A type of small, nylon-string guitar.

Resonator guitar *(95)* A guitar with amplifying, metal resonators attached to the top. Dobro is a very famous manufacturer of these instruments, and players sometimes use the name 'Dobro' to describe any resonator guitar.

Rosette *(6, 7, 10, 26)* The decoration around the edge of the soundhole.

Rosewood *(31, 44)* A wood which is often used for fretboards, backs and sides.

Roundback *(27, 65)* A guitar with a rounded back, usually made of fibreglass. Roundbacks are almost always electro-acoustic guitars.

Saddle *(6, 9, 10, 11, 39)* The thin strip that supports the strings, next to the point where they're attached to the bridge. Saddles were originally made of ivory, but are now usually plastic or, on more expensive guitars, bone. Many steel-string guitars have 'compensated saddles' (ones that don't lie at right angles to the strings), which are designed to improve the intonation. See also: *Intonation.*

Scale *(35–36, 88)* The distance between the nut and the saddle. It is this section of each string that vibrates to create the notes.

Semi-acoustic guitar *(92)* A name often used to

describe archtops with built-in pickups.

Semi-solid guitar *(94)* A guitar with an almost solid body.

Set up *(32, 82)* A guitar that is well 'set up' is easier to play and has better intonation. Having your guitar set up by a specialist involves having the action, the intonation, and sometimes the frets, adjusted.

Sides *(6, 7, 10, 44, 97)* The section of a guitar between the top and the back. The sides are always made of two pieces of wood, each one running from the heel to the tail of the body.

Slab-sawn See: *Quarter-sawn.*

Slide guitar *(2, 76–77)* A playing style where the guitarist moves a 'slide' (originally a bottleneck but now a specially made tube) over the strings, instead of, or as well as, fretting them with the fingertips.

Slotted bridge *(65)* A type of bridge on which the strings run through holes that are parallel to the top. They are found on classical guitars and some steel-string guitars (mainly

roundbacks). See also: *Roundback.*

Slotted head See: *Head.*

Solid *(21, 29–30, 43–44, 86, 96, 98)* A solid top consists of two halves that are cut from a single solid block of wood, and creates better sound than a 'laminated top'. Some expensive guitars also have backs and sides made out of solid wood. See also: *Laminated.*

Soundboard Another name for the top of a guitar. See: *Top.*

Soundbox See: *Body.*

Soundhole *(44)* The hole in the top of a guitar. It's placing, size and shape affects the instrument's tone.

Spanish guitar *(2–3)* Another name for a classical guitar. Confusingly, a flamenco guitar is a guitar made in Spain, but it's a different instrument. Also, a guitar doesn't necessarily have to be made in Spain to be referred to as 'Spanish'. See also: *Classical guitar.*

Spruce *(30)* A type of wood often used for the tops of steel-string guitars.

Steel-string guitar *(3, 9–*

11) An acoustic or electro-acoustic guitar with steel strings and a flat top; also known as 'western guitar', 'folk guitar' or 'flattop guitar'. (Guitars with an arched top also use steel strings but aren't described as steel-string guitars.)

String posts See: *Posts*.

String winder *(64–66, 70)* A tool to speed up the loosening and tightening of strings. Some models have a notch for removing bridge pins.

Strings *(8, 11, 51–60)*; **changing strings** *(60–67)*.

Student guitar *(22–23)* See: *Concert guitar*.

Thumbpick See: *Fingerpicks*.

Top *(6, 7, 10, 11, 21, 29–30, 43–44, 56, 86, 96–97)* The top of the body; also known as the 'soundboard'.

Transducer See: *Pickup*.

Treble strings, trebles See: *Plain strings*.

Triple-0 *(91)* A type of steel-string guitar; 'Double-0' and 'Single-0' models are the next sizes down.

Truss rod *(10, 11, 32, 37, 82)*

An adjustable rod, usually made of metal, that reinforces (trusses) the neck of a steel-string guitar.

Tuner Another name for machine head. However, electronic tuners are often referred to as 'tuners' too. See: *Machine heads* and *Electronic tuner*.

Tuning fork *(69)* A two-pronged metal fork, which creates a note to tune to. Usually available for the notes A, E and C.

Tuning machine See: *Machine heads*.

Twelve-fret neck *(32)* A guitar with a twelve-fret neck is one where the neck meets the body underneath the twelfth fret. A twelve-fret neck does *not* only have twelve frets (because the fretboard continues over the body). Classical guitars, and some steel-string guitars, have twelve-fret necks. See also: *Fourteen-fret neck*.

Twelve-string guitar *(4, 74, 93)* A guitar with six pairs of strings instead of six single strings. They are almost always steel-string guitars, but nylon-string versions do exist (see next page).

Upper bout *(7–10)* The

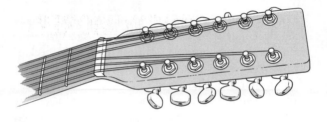

The head of a twelve-string guitar

upper, broader part of the body.

Varnish *(25–26, 44, 83, 98)* The type and quality of varnish used on a guitar can influence both its sound and appearance. Different types of varnishes should be cleaned in different ways.

Waist *(7)* The narrow part of the body.

Watt RMS *(49)* There are various ways of measuring wattage (electrical power). For guitar amps the RMS system is normally used – a '50-watt guitar amp' will have a power of '50 watts RMS'. This may be more power (and volume) than a hi-fi amplifier of '50 watts'.

Western guitar Another name for a steel-string guitar. See: *Steel-string guitar.*

Wood *(30)* The type and quality of wood used to make a guitar greatly affects its sound.

Wound strings *(8, 9, 52–54, 59, 61, 62)* Strings that are wound with thin metal wire. Classical guitars have three wound strings (the thickest three: E, A and D). Steel-string guitars usually have four wound strings (the thickest four: E, A, D and G), but sometimes only have three. Any non-wound string is called a *plain string.*

X-bracing See: *Bracing.*

WANT TO KNOW MORE?

This book gives you all the basics you need for buying, maintaining and using an acoustic guitar. If you want to know more, try the magazines, books, Web sites and newsgroups listed below.

MAGAZINES

Some of these magazines specifically deal with acoustic guitars while others focus mainly on electric instruments but cover acoustics too. Some deal with a specific style of guitar music.

UK
- *Guitarist* guitarist@futurenet.co.uk
- *Classical Guitarist* www.ashleymark.co.uk/classicalguitar.htm

US
- *Acoustic Guitar* www.acguitar.com
- *Fingerstyle Guitar* www.fingerstyleguitar.com
- *Flatpicking* www.flatpick.com
- *Guitar* www.guitarmag.com
- *Guitar Player* www.guitarplayer.com
- *Guitar Review* www.guitarreview.com
- *Guitar Shop* www.guitarshopmag.com
- *Guitar World* www.guitarworld.com
- *Guitar World Acoustic* www.guitarworld.com

CANADA
- *Acoustic Musician* www.netshop.net/acoustic

BOOKS

Countless books on guitars have been written, including some about specific brands like *The Martin Book* and *The Gibson Book*. The three below are good supplements to this guide:

- *The Guitar Handbook*, Ralph Denyer (Dorling Kindersley, UK/US). Includes up-to-date and historical information on electric and acoustic guitars, bass guitars, amplifiers, and recording and effects equipment. It also offers buying advice and technical maintenance tips, and includes a basic playing course covering finger positions, chords, etc.
- *The Complete Guitarist*, Richard Chapman (Dorling Kindersley, UK/US). This book also deals with both electric and acoustic guitars. It contains beautiful pictures, a historical survey, playing tips, tuning tips, exercises, amplification and background information.
- *Acoustic Guitars and Other Fretted Instruments*, Georg Gruhn and Walter Carter (Miller Freeman, US). Historical overview with lots of pictures of special acoustic guitars.

THE INTERNET

The Internet offers a huge amount of information about guitars. One of the easiest ways to discover what's there is to go to a site that offers lots of links to other sites, such as www.guitarsite.com and www.guitarist.com. Lots of brands have their own Web site, which you can often find by putting the brand's name between 'www.' and '.com' (for example, www.gibson.com or www.fender.com). You'll find lots of other sites by doing a Web-search for 'acoustic+guitar'. Many music magazines (see previous page) can also be found on the Internet.

Newsgroups

You can pick up a lot of information in the various guitar newsgroups. Try the following to start off with:

- rec.music.makers.guitar.acoustic
- rec.music.classical.guitar

and for more technical playing tips:

- rec.music.makers.guitar.tablature

ESSENTIAL DATA

In the event of your equipment being stolen or lost, both the police and your insurance company will need certain information. Even if you just want to sell any equipment, it is useful to have a note of the original price and specifications. You can use the space below to keep a record of all the relevant data.

INSURANCE

Company:

Phone: Fax:

Agent:

Phone: Fax:

Policy number:

Premium:

INSTRUMENTS AND ACCESSORIES

Make and model:

Serial number:

Value:

Specifications:

Date of purchase:

Place of purchase:

Phone: Fax:

Make and model:

Serial number:

Value:

Specifications:

Date of purchase:

Place of purchase:

Phone: Fax:

Make and model:

Serial number:

Value:

Specifications:

Date of purchase:

Place of purchase:

Phone: Fax:

STRINGS

If you find some strings that you particularly like, make a
note of the brand, series and gauge/tension here, so you can
use them again:

Brand	Type	Gauge/Tension

ADDITIONAL NOTES

....

....

....

....

....

....

....

....

....

....

....

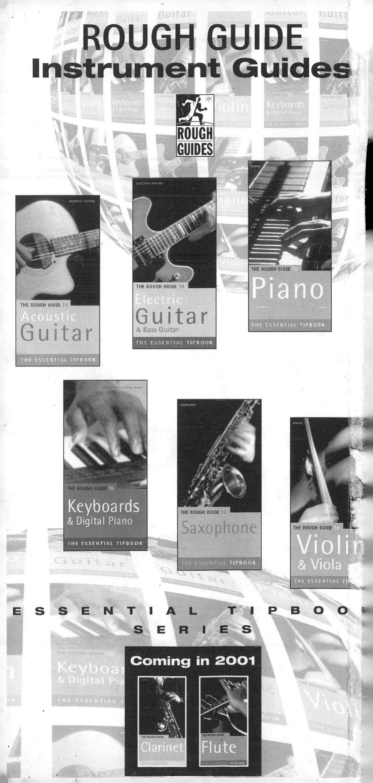

ROUGH GUIDE
Music Books
Music Reference Guides

Essential CD Guides

Mini Guides